I0171820

"Wisdom That Transforms. Action That Lasts."

The Get Wisdom Commitment

At Get Wisdom Publishing we believe that true wisdom has the power to transform lives. Our mission is to equip readers with timeless insights and practical tools that inspire growth, guide decisions, and empower purposeful living. We don't just inform—we empower.

Our books combine profound understanding with real-life application, enabling readers to unlock their potential and navigate life's challenges with clarity and confidence. With each step guided by wisdom, we help you create lasting change and live the life you deserve.

When wisdom meets purpose, transformation follows.

Copyright

ISBN 978-1-952359-62-0   (paperback)
ISBN 978-1-952359-63-7   (ebook)

This book is available as an audiobook on our Amazon Jesus Follower Series page:

Unlock Biblical Wisdom and Transform Your Faith

**For more information
about the Jesus Follower Bible Study Series:**
https://getwisdompublishing.com/jesus-follower-series/

Jesus Follower Bible Study Series

The ONE ANOTHER INSTRUCTIONS to a Jesus Follower

Are You Right With One Another?

Stephen H Berkey

GETWISDOM
PUBLISHING

This book is available as an audiobook on our Amazon Jesus Follower Series page:	

Free PDF

Living Wisely
The Life Planning Guide

A Quick-Start Guide to Purposeful Living and Wise Decisions!

Discover the five life domains: purpose, people, principles, productivity, and perspective. Wisdom is the ability to apply truth and logic to real-life decisions and produce good outcomes. It influences your choices and will produce action that lasts. Consider and apply the five practical wisdom principles for daily living. (6 pages)

Free PDF: https://getwisdompublishing.com/resource-registration/

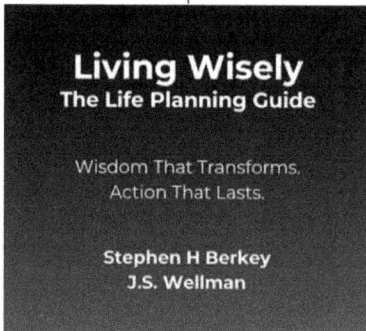

Living Wisely
The Life Planning Guide

Wisdom That Transforms.
Action That Lasts.

Stephen H Berkey
J.S. Wellman

Free PDF

Five Practical Principles For Life

When wisdom meets purpose, transformation follows.

Free PDF
Wise Decision-Making
[Get the ebook version for 99 cents]

You can make good choices.

This free resource provides a project-oriented perspective and gives ten detailed steps to analyze issues/problems to determine a solution. (26 pages)

Good decisions expand your horizons. Don't allow the fear of decision-making paralyze your ability to make good choices. Think through the reasonable alternatives and move forward. When your eyes are on the goal, making good decisions is easier.

Free PDF: https://getwisdompublishing.com/resource-registration/

Kindle ebook for 99 cents: https://www.amazon.com/dp/B09SYGWRVL/

Ebook

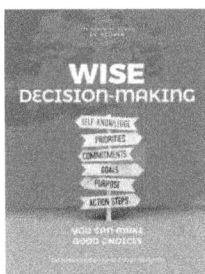

Free PDF

Make Thoughtful Decisions!

Good decisions expand your horizons

Effective Life Change
Applying Biblical Wisdom to Live Your Best Life!

Why Read This Book?

- Transform Your life with Biblical Wisdom.
- Cultivate Practical Wisdom in Your life.
- Navigate Life with a Perspective on Biblical Truth.
- Unlock the Proverbs of the Bible to Live Your Best Life.
- Change and Transform Your life.

Practical Application: These aren't theology or religious discussions, they're practical tools for everyday living.

Get Your Copy Today!

https://www.amazon.com/dp/1952359732
Available in Hardcover, Paperback, Kindle, and Audiobook.

The Jesus Follower Journey

Jesus Follower Bible Study Series

The Jesus Follower Bible Study Series will provide you with a complete description of the nature, characteristics, obligations, commitments, and responsibilities of a true Jesus follower.

Go to our Amazon Book Series page for your copy:
https://www.amazon.com/dp/B0DHP39P5J

The RELATIONSHIP CHARACTERISTICS of a Jesus Follower:
> Are you right with God?

The ONE ANOTHER INSTRUCTIONS to a Jesus Follower:
> Are you right with one another?

The WORSHIP of a Jesus Follower:
> Is your worship acceptable or in vain?

The PRAYER of a Jesus Follower:
> What Scripture says about unleashing the power of God.

The DANGERS of SIN for a Jesus Follower:
> God HATES sin! He abhors sin!

The FOCUS for a Jesus Follower:
> Keep your eyes fixed on Jesus!

The HEART Requirements of a Jesus Follower:
> Follow with all your heart, mind, body, and soul!

The COMMITMENTS of a Jesus Follower:
> Practical Christian living and discipleship.

The OBEDIENCE Requirements for a Jesus Follower:
> Ignore at your own risk!

A related book to this series is, *Effective Life Change: Applying Biblical Wisdom to Live Your Best Life!* This book offers a practical and powerful guide to help navigate life's challenges.

Table of Contents

Message From the Author

Dear Fellow Christ follower,

Welcome to a journey of faith and discovery.

As the author of this Bible study series, I am excited about the future because I believe this book provides the potential to transform lives, deepen our understanding of God's Word, and ignite a desire within us—a fire that draws us into the presence of our God.

Why read the Jesus Follower Series?

Deeper Roots: We all long for roots that run deep—roots anchored in truth, love, and purpose. In this series, we'll dig into the bedrock of Scripture, unearthing spiritual principles that will guide us in our faith journey.

Authentic Discipleship: Being a Jesus follower isn't about rituals or a superficial commitment. It's about walking the narrow path, picking up your cross, and living a life that loves God, follows Jesus, and loves one another. We will explore what it means to be authentic disciples.

Unveiling Mysteries: God is a source of mysteries and His Word is waiting to be discovered. Together we will examine and encounter the living Word—the One who breathes life into every syllable.

Community and Connection: We are not meant to walk this path alone. As you read, imagine joining a global community of fellow seekers. We will discuss, question, and grow together. Our shared journey will enrich us all. I encourage you to gather friends to join you in this journey.

Expected Benefits:

Renewed Passion: Prepare yourself to wake up each morning with a renewed passion for God's Word. These studies will ignite your hunger for truth and draw you into deeper relationship with the Author of Life.

Practical Application: These aren't theoretical discussions; they're practical tools for everyday living. Expect to see real-life changes—whether it's in your relationships, commitment, or prayer life.

Spiritual Resilience: Life's storms will come, but armed with the insights from God's Word, you can stand firm. Your faith will weather trials, doubts, and uncertainties. You will emerge stronger and more resilient.

Joyful Obedience: As we explore the nature of discipleship, you'll discover that obedience isn't a burden—it's a joy. The path of obedience leads to peace, and you'll find yourself saying, "Yes, Lord!" with newfound delight.

Let's Begin!

So, turn the page. Dive into the first chapter. Let the words seep into your soul. And remember, you're not alone—we're on this pilgrimage together. May these books be more than ink on paper; may they be stepping stones toward a life that leads to eternity. Amen!

"We believe applied wisdom empowers life change. Our books provide clarity, inspiration, and tools to equip readers to live their best life."

My prayer is that you will

Be tenacious like Job
Walk like Enoch
Believe like Abraham
Wrestle like Jacob
Dress like Joseph
Lead like Moses
Conquer like Deborah
Be fearless like Shamgar
Inspire like Josuha
Influence like Esther
Dance like David
Ask like Jabez
Have the faith of Daniel
Pray like Elijah
Trust like Elisha
Commit like Isaiah
Be courageous like Benaiah
Rebuild like Nehemiah
Be obedient like Hosea
Be zealous like Zacchaeus
Surrender like Mary
Stand firm like Stephen
Speak like Peter
Seize opportunities like Philip
Submit like Paul
Overcome like the Elect (Saints)
Worship like the 24 Elders
and
Love like Jesus

Steve

Introduction

Book Description – *Embracing Authentic Community*

Are you truly living out your faith as a Jesus follower? In this book you will embark on a journey of faith that reveals the heart of the Christian life—relationships and community. Loving God is inseparable from loving one another. This compelling Bible study invites you to explore the profound implications of this truth, guiding you through essential teachings on building genuine, Christ-centered relationships with one another.

At the core of Jesus' teachings lies the powerful commandment to love God wholeheartedly and to love one another as ourselves. But what does it really mean to "love" one another in a way that honors God? This book uncovers the essential instructions from Scripture, guiding you to cultivate meaningful relationships that embody the love of Christ.

Through deep exploration of key principles such as encouragement, forgiveness, service, and truth-telling, you will discover how to:

Encourage One Another: Build a supportive community that uplifts and inspires.

Forgive One Another: Learn the liberating power of forgiveness and reconciliation.

Bear Fruit: Understand the fruit of the Spirit that manifest in a life dedicated to Christ.

Love One Another: Love one another like Christ loves you.

Serve One Another: Embrace the joy of serving, reflecting Jesus' humility and love.

Speak Truth to One Another: Foster an atmosphere of honesty and integrity.

Make and Teach Disciples: Answer the call to spread the Gospel and nurture faith in others.

Share Jesus with the World: Equip yourself to be a bold witness of Christ's love.

Each lesson is designed to challenge and inspire you to reflect on your relationships, pushing you to align your actions with your faith. With practical applications and insightful discussions, this study will not only deepen your understanding of what it means to be a true Jesus follower but also empower you to live it out in your daily life.

Are you ready to examine your heart and relationships in light of Christ's teachings? Dive into these lessons and ignite a passion for loving others as He has loved you. Whether you're a seasoned believer or new to the faith, this book offers profound insights and actionable steps to strengthen your relationships and align your life with the teachings of Jesus.

Your journey to being right with God and one another starts here—transform your life today!

Group Discussion or Individual Study

These studies can be done individually or in a small discussion group. An important value of the study is in the discussion questions. We all see life differently and the thoughts and ideas shared in a group will often lead to a richer understanding of the Scripture.

Format of Lessons

The format of the lessons is not the same in each book. We chose a format that best fit the material.

We Reap What We Sow!

In a number of his proverbs, King Solomon suggests that doing what is right is to be preferred over evil. King Solomon was known world-wide for his great wisdom. He wrote and recorded many proverbs recognized for their practical insight and wisdom. He describes the nature of righteousness as being immovable and says that it will stand above evil.

Is your desire for doing what is "right" rooted deeply or is it planted in shallow soil that can easily be washed away? Solomon indicated that the wicked would ultimately be overthrown and that the righteous would survive because their character had roots that were deep and impossible to dislodge.

Solomon argued that it was better to be on the side of the righteous. The reasoning is the same as the man who builds his house, business, or life on rock versus sand. If we build on sand (questionable ways) then our hopes and plans will never stand up against the storms of life. If we build on rock (character, commitment, and obedience) our plans will hold firm.

We do reap what we sow and if we sow badly because we have rejected what is right, the wise counsel of friends, or our core values, we will reap the negative consequences. Those who think they know everything frequently reject wisdom and follow their own plans and schemes. It has been said that those who insist on following their own foolish ways will often end up choking on them.

Lesson 1
A Jesus Follower
ENCOURAGES One Another

PART A – PRAY FOR ONE ANOTHER

*Therefore, confess your sins to one another
and pray for one another, that you may be healed.
The prayer of a righteous person
has great power as it is working.*
James 5:16 ESV

MEDITATION

Meditate on 2 Tim 1:2-8 during your Quiet Time this week.

2 Timothy 1:2-8 *To Timothy, my dear son: Grace, mercy
and peace from God the Father and Christ Jesus our Lord. 3
I thank God, whom I serve, as my forefathers did, with a
clear conscience, as night and day I constantly remember
you in my prayers. 4 Recalling your tears, I long to see you,
so that I may be filled with joy. 5 I have been reminded of
your sincere faith, which first lived in your grandmother
Lois and in your mother Eunice and, I am persuaded, now
lives in you also. 6 For this reason I remind you to fan into
flame the gift of God, which is in you through the laying on
of my hands. 7 For God did not give us a spirit of timidity,*

but a spirit of power, of love and of self-discipline. 8 So do not be ashamed to testify about our Lord, or ashamed of me his prisoner. But join with me in suffering for the gospel, by the power of God. NIV

NOTES:

INTRODUCTION

Note that we have separated this lesson between praying for one another (Part A) and encouraging one another (Part B). Prayer is such a specific activity that we felt it should be treated separately. In addition, there is a specific instruction to pray for one another (James 5:16). However, we will not investigate this subject as deeply as might be warranted since there is a separate book in this Series on prayer: *The PRAYER of a Jesus Follower: What Scripture says about unleashing the power of God*.

In this and the next seven lessons we will examine how the Jesus follower is to relate to other believers and to the world. We must not only have a right relationship with God but a right relationship with the people around us, both believers and unbelievers.

If the relationship with God is not right, then the relationship with other people will not be right either. A right relationship with others should flow out of a right relationship with God. Yes, we can certainly do some good deeds and ministry relying on self, but it will never be what could be accomplished if we are right with God. Our religious activity has meaning or significance only within the context of a love relationship with God through Christ.

Nothing of _eternal value_ can be accomplished if the relationship with God is not right.

Everything God wants to do through me, He will accomplish out of the excess love that flows from the relationship I have with Him.

JESUS' PRAYER – John 17

In John 17 we have the longest recorded prayer of Jesus. In it, He prays for Himself, His disciples, and future believers. It is instructive to look closely at how and what Jesus prays for others:

John 17:11   . . . _protect them by the power of your name, the name you gave me so that they may be one as we are one._

John 17:15   _My prayer is not that you take them out of the world but that you protect them from the evil one._

John 17:17   _Sanctify them by the truth; your word is truth._

John 17:21   _That all of them may be one, Father, just as you are in me and I am in you. May they also be in us so that the world may believe that you have sent me._

John 17:23   _I in them and you in me. May they be brought to complete unity to let the world know that you sent me and have loved them even as you have loved me._

John 17:24   _Father, I want those you have given me to be with me where I am, and to see my glory, the glory you have given me because you loved me before the creation of the world._ NIV

Q1. Record the different things Jesus prayed for his disciples and future believers in John 17 above.

His Disciples:
17:11

17:15

17:17

Future Believers:
17:21a

17:21b

17:23

17:24a

17:24b

Q2. What is the theme of Jesus' prayer for future believers?

Q3. In your words, what does that mean?

PAUL'S PRAYERS

Colossians 1:9-12
And so, from the day we heard, we have not ceased to pray for you, asking that you may be filled with the knowledge of his will in all spiritual wisdom and understanding, 10 so as to walk in a manner worthy of the Lord, fully pleasing to

him, bearing fruit in every good work and increasing in the knowledge of God. 11 May you be strengthened with all power, according to his glorious might, for all endurance and patience with joy, 12 giving thanks to the Father, who has qualified you to share in the inheritance of the saints in light. ESV

Q4. Record the different things Paul prayed for believers at Colossae in Colossians 1:9-12.

1:9

1:10a

1:10b

1:11

1:12

Q5. Which one of these prayers of Jesus and Paul would mean the most to you if someone prayed them for you? Why?

Q6. Do you personally believe that God will change or transform somebody's life if you intercede for them? Explain.

Ephesians 3:14-21

For this reason I bow my knees before the Father, 15 from whom every family in heaven and on earth is named, 16 that according to the riches of his glory he may grant you to be strengthened with power through his Spirit in your inner being, 17 so that Christ may dwell in your hearts through faith—that you, being rooted and grounded in love, 18 may have strength to comprehend with all the saints what is the breadth and length and height and depth, 19 and to know the love of Christ that surpasses knowledge, that you may be filled with all the fullness of God. 20 Now to him who is able to do far more abundantly than all that we ask or think, according to the power at work within us, 21 to him be glory in the church and in Christ Jesus throughout all generations, forever and ever. Amen. ESV

Q7. In Ephesians 3:16 Paul prays that the inner being would be strengthened with power. What does Paul mean by "inner being?"

Q8. What is the request Paul makes on behalf of the believers in Ephesians 3:17a – 19a?

Q9. What does Paul say will be a result of this (Ephesians 3:19b) and what does it mean?

RESULT:

MEANING:

Q10. What is the nature of the prayers of Jesus and Paul quoted above? How would you classify, categorize, or describe them? What is their significance?

NATURE:

DESCRIPTION:

PERSONAL APPLICATION

Given the prayers of Jesus and Paul, how do you need to pray differently?

WHAT I WANT TO REMEMBER

Enter some notes and information that you want to remember about this lesson. It might be a Scripture verse or two, something new you learned, something you want to do, something you want to change, or just something you want to be sure to remember.

Wisdom to Action
Challenge

Who in your life needs intercessory prayer right now? How can you commit to praying for them consistently this week, and what specific needs will you bring before God on their behalf?

PART B – ENCOURAGE ONE ANOTHER

*Therefore encourage one another and build
one another up, just as you are doing.*
1 Thessalonians 5:11 ESV

Encouraging someone means you are making them more determined, hopeful, or confident about themselves or something else. It could include inspiring someone toward an objective or goal.

PAUL's INSTRUCTIONS

Hebrews 3:13 *But exhort one another every day, as long as it is called "today," that none of you may be hardened by the deceitfulness of sin.* ESV

Hebrews 10:25 *not neglecting to meet together, as is the habit of some, but encouraging one another, and all the more as you see the Day drawing near.* ESV

Q1. Based on Heb 3:13, why are we to encourage one another?

Q2. What does being hardened mean?

HOW TO ENCOURAGE OTHERS

Matthew 14:27 *But immediately Jesus spoke to them, saying, "Take heart; it is I. Do not be afraid."* ESV

Hebrews 6:18 *so that by two unchangeable things, in which it is impossible for God to lie, we who have fled for refuge might have strong encouragement to hold fast to the hope set before us.* ESV

Hebrews 12:5 *And have you forgotten the exhortation that addresses you as sons? "My son, do not regard lightly the discipline of the Lord, nor be weary when reproved by him."* ESV

2 Timothy 1:15-18 *You are aware that all who are in Asia turned away from me, among whom are Phygelus and Hermogenes. 16 May the Lord grant mercy to the household of Onesiphorus, for he often refreshed me and was not ashamed of my chains, 17 but when he arrived in Rome he searched for me earnestly and found me— 18 may the Lord grant him to find mercy from the Lord on that Day!—and you well know all the service he rendered at Ephesus.* ESV

Q3. What are examples of Paul's encouraging words in 2 Timothy 1:16-18 above?

1:16

1:16

1:17

1:18

1:18

OBSERVATION

Q4. What do the following Scriptures say about <u>how</u> and <u>why</u> to encourage one another?

Romans 1:11-12 *I long to see you so that I may impart to you some spiritual gift to make you strong that is, that you and I may be mutually encouraged by each other's faith.* NIV

HOW:

WHY:

Titus 1:9 *He must hold firmly to the trustworthy message as it has been taught, so that he can encourage others by sound doctrine and refute those who oppose it.* NIV

HOW:

WHY:

Colossians 2:1-2a *I want you to know how much I am struggling {praying} for you . . .   2 My purpose is that they may be encouraged in heart and united in love,* NIV

HOW:

WHY:

Q5. In your world what gets in the way of praying for and encouraging others? What are the hindrances or distractions that you battle?

Q6. What would reduce or lessen the distractions?

SELF REFLECTION

To what degree are you currently a prayer warrior or encourager? How would you evaluate your situation after examining the nature of your personal prayer life and degree of encouragement for others?

CONCLUSION

In 1 Thessalonians we observe Paul's words of encouragement:

> 2:12   urging you to live lives worthy of God . . .
> 5:11   to build each other up . . .
> 5:14   to encourage the timid, help the weak, and be patient with everyone

Paul was not timid in either his exhortation or his encouragement. We need to hear these words and do the same. We should live lives that are worthy while building up and encouraging each other.

Who could you encourage today? _____

Paul also was encouraged by the faith of others and sent disciples (like Timothy) to churches to encourage them in their faith. Our encouragement can be physical, mental, or emotional. But, whatever the purpose we should always encourage others in their faith.

There is no better encouragement than knowing someone is praying for you. How would you feel knowing that before you rise from your bed someone has taken your name before the throne of God. If that is meaningful to you, consider doing that for others.

SUGGESTED PERSONAL PRAYER

Spouse: Father, work in and through __(spouse)__ and lead them in glorifying You. Give them wisdom and understanding and thoughts that will build them up and encourage them and those around them. Pour out Your blessings on them in all areas of their life.

Family: Lord, I pray that our home would be a place of peace, love, and respect; that we would think of each other's needs before our own.

Friend: Lord, please bring encouragement into __X's___ life. Cause them to be inspired and motivated in their faith. Expand their relationship with Christ so that You are honored.

My Prayer

What I Want to Remember

Enter some notes and information that you want to remember about this lesson. It might be a Scripture verse or two, something new you learned, something you want to do, something you want to change, or just something you want to be sure to remember.

Wisdom to Action
Challenge

Think of someone in your faith community who might be struggling. What specific act of encouragement can you offer them this week to strengthen their faith and promote unity?

Lesson 2
A Jesus Follower
FORGIVES One Another

MEDITATATION

Meditate on Psalm 32:1-5 during your Quiet Time this week.

Psalms 32:1-5 *Blessed is the one whose transgression is <u>forgiven</u>, whose sin is covered. 2 Blessed is the man against whom the Lord counts no iniquity, and in whose spirit there is no deceit. 3 For when I kept silent, my bones wasted away through my groaning all day long. 4 For day and night your hand was heavy upon me; my strength was dried up as by the heat of summer. Selah 5 I acknowledged my sin to you, and I did not cover my iniquity; I said, "I will <u>confess</u> my transgressions to the Lord," and you <u>forgave</u> the iniquity of my sin. Selah. ESV*

NOTES:

INTRODUCTION

Some years ago a middle-aged woman sought to be reunited in marriage with her former husband. She told her pastor that they were both Christians when they were married, and that they had two sons. One day they quarreled and harsh words were spoken. Each was too proud to ask for the other's forgiveness, and the bitter feelings led to a divorce. Neither had remarried.

Twenty-five years later, with one son dead and the whereabouts of the other unknown, the woman learned that the only man she had ever really loved was in the hospital. She went to see him, and with tears they forgave one another. At their request, the pastor gladly remarried them right there in the hospital room.

As he left after performing the ceremony, the pastor thought of the price they had paid because of their unwillingness to forgive. They were not able to experience the joy of their salvation and their sons had suffered because of a broken home. Although the husband and the wife were now reunited there had been many wasted years that could never be relived.

Anybody who harbors an unforgiving spirit is cheating himself of fellowship with God and the ability to serve God and others. No one should pay the price of bearing a grudge![1]

The Lord said, "*but if you do not forgive others their trespasses, neither will your Father forgive your trespasses.* (Matthew 6:15 ESV) Jesus is telling us that if we refuse to forgive there may be serious consequences. An unforgiving spirit and an unwillingness to grant pardon appears to be a sin that lasts into eternity! It can certainly destroy the ability to live in peace and rest in this life. Don't miss that

Jesus said, "neither will your Father (God) forgive your trespasses."

Forgiveness in the non-biblical sense means one ceases feeling angry with another. We simply choose to ignore resentment and not blame someone for a trespass. The offense is excused.

From God's perspective, forgiveness refers to God pardoning man's sins. Remember, sin is rebellion against His laws and instructions.

Some may suggest that the Biblical definition of forgiveness is the process of forgiving one another for the sins someone commits against us. Do you think that is true? [This might be a trick question ☺]

Q1. What thoughts, concepts, actions, or images do you personally think of when you hear the word "forgiveness?"

a)

b)

c)

d)

Q2. When one says they cannot forgive, who are they trying to punish?

Unfortunately the one who is really punished is the one refusing to forgive. The one who hurt you may not know or care about what you think about the situation that caused the hurt. Your bitterness not only hurts you but often many of your other relationships

COMMANDED TO FORGIVE

Ephesians 4:32 *Be kind to one another, tenderhearted, forgiving one another, as God in Christ forgave you.* ESV

Colossians 3:13 *bearing with one another and, if one has a complaint against another, forgiving each other; as the Lord has forgiven you, so you also must forgive.* ESV

Q3. Based on the above, why should we forgive someone who seriously offends or hurts us?

Q4. Do you think that the reasons given above for forgiving another person are sufficient reasons to forgive?

Any discussion about forgiveness always raises the question of how many times one should forgive if the offender repeats the offense. Jesus answered that question when He said every time:

Luke 17:4 *and if he sins against you seven times in the day, and turns to you seven times, saying, 'I repent,' you must forgive him.* ESV

Christ taught that forgiveness is a duty. No limit should be set on the extent of forgiveness, and it must be granted without reserve. The forgiveness principle cannot be reduced to a formula.

Q5. Forgiving a significant offense once is challenging enough, but how many of us are willing to forgive someone who continually offends? Why do you think God asks us to do this?

WARNING and JUDGMENT!

Forgiveness is a unique relationship characteristic because there are so many warnings against un-forgiveness. The Bible says we are to forgive and spends a great deal of time warning the reader what will happen if we do <u>not</u> forgive.

Q6. What is the warning or the judgment described in the following passages?

Matthew 6:14-15 *For if you forgive others their trespasses, your heavenly Father will also forgive you, 15 but if you do not forgive others their trespasses, neither will your Father forgive your trespasses.* ESV

Mark 11:25-26 *And whenever you stand praying, forgive, if you have anything against anyone, so that your Father also who is in heaven may forgive you your trespasses.* ESV

Luke 6:37-38 *Judge not, and you will not be judged; condemn not, and you will not be condemned; forgive, and you will be forgiven; 38 give, and it will be given to you. Good measure, pressed down, shaken together, running over, will be put into your lap. For with the measure you use it will be measured back to you.* ESV

Romans 12:17 *Repay no one evil for evil, but give thought to do what is honorable in the sight of all.* ESV

What would it take to motivate you to forgive? Are the above warnings strong enough to motivate you personally to forgive in all circumstances? Does this type of motivation work for you?

Q7. What would it take to make forgiveness a natural part of your life?

PARABLE OF UNMERCIFUL SERVANT

Matthew 18:23-35 *Therefore the kingdom of heaven may be compared to a king who wished to settle accounts with his servants. 24 When he began to settle, one was brought to him who owed him ten thousand talents. 25 And since he could not pay, his master ordered him to be sold, with*

his wife and children and all that he had, and payment to be made. 26 So the servant fell on his knees, imploring him, 'Have patience with me, and I will pay you everything.' 27 And out of pity for him, the master of that servant released him and forgave him the debt. 28 But when that same servant went out, he found one of his fellow servants who owed him a hundred denarii, and seizing him, he began to choke him, saying, 'Pay what you owe.' 29 So his fellow servant fell down and pleaded with him, 'Have patience with me, and I will pay you.' 30 He refused and went and put him in prison until he should pay the debt. 31 When his fellow servants saw what had taken place, they were greatly distressed, and they went and reported to their master all that had taken place. 32 Then his master summoned him and said to him, 'You wicked servant! I forgave you all that debt because you pleaded with me. 33 And should not you have had mercy on your fellow servant, as I had mercy on you?' 34 And in anger his master delivered him to the jailers, until he should pay all his debt. 35 So also my heavenly Father will do to every one of you, if you do not forgive your brother from your heart. ESV

Q8. What is the purpose of this parable?

Q9. What is the primary teaching of this parable?

Q10. Is 18:35 part of the parable or a separate warning?

Assuming we are describing what the "Kingdom" is like, does this parable mean such a person does not get into the Kingdom? Or is he thrown out of the Kingdom? Or is he thrown into prison in the Kingdom? Or does it just teach we are to forgive and the punishment is only to demonstrate how serious God is about forgiving?

Q11. What do you understand this parable to mean?

CHURCH DISCIPLINE

2 Corinthians 2:6-11 *For such a one, this punishment by the majority is enough, 7 so you should rather turn to forgive and comfort him, or he may be overwhelmed by excessive sorrow. 8 So I beg you to reaffirm your love for him. 9 For this is why I wrote, that I might test you and know whether you are obedient in everything. 10 Anyone whom you forgive, I also forgive. What I have forgiven, if I have forgiven anything, has been for your sake in the presence of Christ, 11 so that we would not be outwitted by Satan; for we are not ignorant of his designs.* ESV

Q12. What is the real issue in 2 Corinthians 2:6-11?

The story above is about a person who has committed a serious sin and the Christian community at Corinth has exercised appropriate church discipline. But after the offender has repented and shown genuine sorrow for the sin, the discipline or punishment is not lifted. The person is not restored to the community as he should be. Discipline cannot be allowed to be imposed without room for grace and restoration. Remember Jesus said: *"Pay attention to yourselves! If your brother sins, rebuke him, and if he repents, forgive him."* (Lk 17:3 ESV)

BIBLICAL EXAMPLES

Q13. Can you think of a story, parable, or situation in the Old Testament, not already mentioned above, that illustrates forgiving one another? [Need help? Think about Esau, Joseph, Moses, David, or Solomon.]

1.

2.

3.

4.

5.

PERSONAL REFLECTION

Q14. Is there someone in your life today whom you have not truly forgiven?

If so, write their name or names below. If the nature of the offense requires you to tell them, write a deadline for accomplishing that.

Name(s)   Date/Deadline

_____   _____

_____   _____

CONCLUSION

The hope or goal of forgiveness should be to restore a relationship to its former condition. Such restoration normally requires the cooperation of both parties. However, full restoration is not always possible. Our responsibility is to forgive. We have no control over the response of the other party.

What are the rewards for a forgiving spirit? Matthew 5:7 says that the merciful will receive mercy and be blessed. The most important reward or result from forgiving another may be that we avoid bondage. Holding a grudge can enslave one in bitterness, hostility, and resentment. We must be aware of our words and actions so that "*no one misses the grace of God and that no bitter root grows up to cause trouble and defile many*." (Hebrews 12:15)

The subject of forgiveness is so important to Christ that it is included in His model prayer: "Forgive us our sins, as we have forgiven those who have sinned against us." Our spirit should reflect a conscience attitude of forgiveness. We should automatically forgive others because it is in our Christian DNA. We should respond to others who offend us, regardless of the nature of that offense. It is likely a minor infraction when compared to the infinite debt that Jesus paid for us. We have been given a gift of grace we do not deserve. We have been given eternal life. How can we in good conscience refuse to forgive another?

Do you have bitterness in your heart toward someone? Are you holding a grudge? Is there someone in your life whom you have refused to forgive? As a friend of mine would say, "Get over it!" The one you are hurting is yourself. It does not really matter how the other person responds. The freedom is gained when you forgive.

The three most important characteristics of a person who truly forgives those who offend them might be the following:

1. They have a strong relationship with Christ.

2. They have a humble spirit, putting others first.

3. They truly understand what Christ did for them.

Prayer

Lord, empower me to forgive all those who offend me. Do not allow me to carry bitterness and resentment in my heart. Free me from the bondage of un-forgiveness.

My Prayer

What I Want to Remember

Enter some notes and information that you want to remember about this lesson. It might be a Scripture verse or two, something new you learned, something you want to do, something you want to change, or just something you want to be sure to remember.

Wisdom to Action
Challenge

Is there someone you need to forgive? What step can you take today to begin the process of forgiveness, reflecting God's mercy in your own life?

Lesson 3
A Jesus Follower is
FRUITFUL

MEDITATION

Meditate on Romans 7:4 during your Quiet Time this week.

Romans 7:4 *Likewise, my brothers, you also have died to the law through the body of Christ, so that you may belong to another, to him who has been raised from the dead, in order that we may bear <u>fruit</u> for God.* ESV

NOTES:

INTRODUCTION

The "fruit" image in the Bible is used symbolically to represent something that you or I do that results in or produces something. It could be good fruit or bad fruit.

The imagery is used in several ways but probably the most important is the character traits that God refers to as "*The Fruit of the Spirit.*" These are outlined in Galatians 5:22-23:

love, joy, peace, patience, kindness, goodness, faithfulness, gentleness, and self-control.

In Ephesians 5:9 Paul refers to character traits as fruit of the light consisting of goodness, righteousness and truth. These are traits that God is producing in us during the process of transforming us into the likeness of Christ.

Another use of this term refers to the results of our walk with God. My life will produce results from my actions (and inaction) that result from my relationship or lack of relationship with Christ. The imagery is particularly strong in John 15 when Jesus states, "I am the true vine." He then goes on to describe why a Jesus follower needs to stay connected to Christ: to produce fruit.

THE NATURE OF FRUIT

Fruit has a very important function as described in the following passages. Note what it represents in the following two passages:

Matthew 7:16 By their fruit you will recognize them. . . . NIV

Matthew 12:33 Make a tree good and its fruit will be good, or make a tree bad and its fruit will be bad, for a tree is recognized by its fruit. NIV

In Matthew 7:16 we are told that the fruit allows us to identify or recognize true believers. Matthew 12:33 expands on this truth by indicating the fruit can be good or bad and in that way we can identify believers because they will normally produce good fruit.

Q1. How is fruit described or defined in the following passages?

Philippians 1:11 *filled with the fruit of righteousness that comes through Jesus Christ, to the glory and praise of God.* ESV

Hebrews 13:15-16 *Through him then let us continually offer up a sacrifice of praise to God, that is, the fruit of lips that acknowledge his name. 16 Do not neglect to do good and to share what you have, for such sacrifices are pleasing to God.* ESV

Colossians 1:6 *which has come to you, as indeed in the whole world it is bearing fruit and growing—as it also does among you, since the day you heard it and understood the grace of God in truth.* ESV

GOOD and BAD FRUIT

Q2. How is _good_ fruit described in the following passages?

Matthew 3:8 *Bear <u>fruit</u> in keeping with repentance.* ESV

Matthew 21:43 *Therefore I tell you, the kingdom of God will be taken away from you and given to a people producing its <u>fruits</u>.* ESV

James 3:17 *But the wisdom from above is first pure, then peaceable, gentle, open to reason, full of mercy and good fruits, impartial and sincere.* ESV

Colossians 1:10 *so as to walk in a manner worthy of the Lord, fully pleasing to him, bearing fruit in every good work and increasing in the knowledge of God.* ESV

Q3. How is *bad* fruit described in the following passages?

Matthew 3:10 *Even now the axe is laid to the root of the trees. Every tree therefore that does not bear good fruit is cut down and thrown into the fire.* ESV

Matthew 21:19 *And seeing a fig tree by the wayside, he went to it and found nothing on it but only leaves. And he said to it, "May no fruit ever come from you again!" And the fig tree withered at once.* ESV

Q4. In Matthew 3:10 and 21:9 what makes the fruit bad?

Q5. What do you think is the most important concept to remember about good or bad fruit?

PURPOSE OF FRUIT

Based on the following, our good deeds (fruit) are to point people to God.

> **Matthew 5:16** *In the same way, let your light shine before others, so that they may see your good works and give glory to your Father who is in heaven.* ESV
> **1 Peter 2:12** *Keep your conduct among the Gentiles honorable, so that when they speak against you as evildoers, they may see your good deeds and glorify God on the day of visitation.* ESV

Is this your experience? Has your fruit caused someone to recognize Christ in you? Has someone else praised God because of what you did or said? Do you have a testimony to share that would be meaningful to your group?

Q6. What do you learn about fruit in the following?

John 15:16 ESV *You did not choose me, but I chose you and appointed you that you should go and bear fruit and that your fruit should abide, so that whatever you ask the Father in my name, he may give it to you.*
John 15:16 NLT *You didn't choose me. I chose you. I appointed you to go and produce lasting fruit, so that the Father will give you whatever you ask for, using my name.*

Note: In John 15:16 above the ESV indicates that the fruit should "abide." In the NLT and some other translations the word "lasting" is used. It may imply the reference is to making disciples. Regardless, the meaning clearly is that one is to bear fruit that is productive and consistent with the purposes of God.

John 15:8 *By this my Father is glorified, that you <u>bear much fruit</u> and so prove to be my disciples.* ESV

Matthew 21:43 *Therefore I tell you, the kingdom of God will be taken away from you and given to a people <u>producing its fruits</u>.* ESV

PARABLE – Fig Tree

In Luke 3, the author has just reported that John the Baptist was preaching a message of "repentance for the forgiveness of sins" and then he says:

> **Luke 3:8-9** *<u>Bear fruits</u> in keeping with repentance. And do not begin to say to yourselves, 'We have Abraham as our father.' For I tell you, God is able from these stones to raise up children for Abraham. 9 Even now the axe is laid to the root of the trees. Every tree therefore that does not bear <u>good fruit</u> is cut down and thrown into the fire.* ESV

At the beginning of Luke 13 the author is again talking about repentance and before recording the parable of the fig tree, he says, "unless you repent, you will all likewise perish."

Luke 13: 6-9 The Parable of the Barren Fig Tree:
And he told this parable: "A man had a fig tree planted in his vineyard, and he came seeking fruit on it and found none. 7 And he said to the vinedresser, 'Look, for three years now I have come seeking fruit on this fig tree, and I find none. Cut it down. Why should it use up the ground?' 8 And he answered him, 'Sir, let it alone this year also, until I dig around it and put on manure. 9 Then if it should bear fruit next year, well and good; but if not, you can cut it down.'" ESV

Q7. Use any and all resources available to you and determine who or what each of the following parts of the parable represent?

a. OWNER:

b. VINEYARD:

c. FIG TREE: *individual soul*
NOTE: It could also be argued that the fig tree is Israel, but for our purposes, we will assume it is personal.

d. COMING OF OWNER:

e. BARRENNESS:

f. VINEDRESSER:

g. DELAY:

h. "CUT IT DOWN:"

Q8. What were the two reasons the tree was to be cut down?

Q9. What is the reason the tree should have a place in the vineyard for no purpose?

Q10. Why the urgency?

Q11. What is the point of each word below relative to this parable?

a. *patience*:

b. *opportunity:*

c. *uselessness:*

d. *use of resources*:

e. *time*:

f. *judgment*:

g. *expectation*:

Q12. How would you relate the Parable of the Talents (Matthew 25:14-30) to this parable?

HINDRANCES

Q. In the real world (in your life) what gets in the way of producing fruit?

Q. What would lessen the distractions or make them go away for you?

CONCLUSION

When I think of "fruit" my mind automatically goes to the Fruit of the Spirit and good deeds. But these are actually dramatically different kinds of fruit.

The Fruit of the Spirit represents my character, and, although I can and should work at it, most of the change and improvement comes through God and the working of the Holy Spirit in my life.

Good deeds and sharing my testimony, on the other hand, come from activity that I do as the result of the relationship I have with Christ. As that relationship deepens I am likely to do more and more and do it better and better.

If my relationship with God is not right, it will be difficult to have much fruit of either kind.

If you are not satisfied with the quantity or quality of your fruit, work on your relationship with Jesus. Fruit will come when you are growing in your relationship with Christ. It will come out of the overflow of that relationship. If you are not spending time with God, growing in your knowledge of God, and walking in humility with Him, it will be difficult to produce any kind of meaningful fruit.

The relationship with God must be right so that the relationship with others can occur.

Prayer
Lord, allow the fruit in my life to point toward Jesus.

My Prayer

What I Want to Remember

Enter some notes and information that you want to remember about this lesson. It might be a Scripture verse or two, something new you learned, something you want to do, something you want to change, or just something you want to be sure to remember.

Wisdom to Action
Challenge

Reflect on your life. Which fruit of the Spirit do you feel is lacking? How can you more intentionally abide in Christ this week to cultivate this fruit?

Lesson 4
A Jesus Follower
LOVES ONE ANOTHER

. . .Which commandment is the most important of all?. . .
Love the Lord your God with all your heart, . . .
The second is: Love your neighbor as yourself.
There is no other commandment greater than these.
Mark 12:28-31

MEDITATION

Meditate on the *importance* of agape love during your Quiet Time this week.

Galatians 5:6 *For in Christ Jesus neither circumcision nor uncircumcision counts for anything, but only faith working through love.* ESV

AGAPE LOVE

Agape love is a decision or choice of the heart; it is powered by your will. It is self-giving and, like humility, it puts the needs of others before one's own needs. *Agape* describes a love that comes from or is rooted in a relationship with God and it is unconditional! I *agape* love even though the loved one may be unkind, unlovely, unworthy, or has said something unkind. *Agape* determines to do whatever is best for the loved one. I willingly sacrifice myself for another's need. *Agape* gives when it gets nothing in return. It does not think of getting something back.

AGAPE LOVE COMES FROM GOD

Whatever love exists in man has its origin in God, whether it is directed back to God, or toward family, friends, or neighbors. God is working in us to produce fruit, good deeds, acts of grace, all to bring glory to Himself.

1 John 4:7 *Beloved, let us <u>love one another</u>, for love is from God, and whoever loves has been born of God and knows God.* ESV

1 John 4:12 *No one has ever seen God; if we <u>love one another</u>, God abides in us and his love is perfected in us.* ESV

1 John 4:19 *We <u>love</u> because he first loved us.* ESV

Q1. What is meant or implied by the statement "love comes from God"?

Q2. What kind of activities in your life take priority over "loving one another?" List three:

1.

2.

3.

If you are having trouble with self-examination, think about the reasons why <u>other people</u> are not very loving! ☺

LOVING ONE ANOTHER

Q3. What do you learn about *agape* love in the following:

1 John 3:10 *By this it is evident who are the children of God, and who are the children of the devil: whoever does not practice righteousness is not of God, nor is the one who does not love his brother.* ESV

1 John 3:14-15 *We know that we have passed out of death into life, because we love the brothers. Whoever does not love abides in death. 15 Everyone who hates his brother is a murderer, and you know that no murderer has eternal life abiding in him.* ESV

1 John 4:11-12 *Beloved, if God so loved us, we also ought to love one another. 12 No one has ever seen God; if we love one another, God abides in us and his love is perfected in us.* ESV

1 John 4:20-21 *If anyone says, "I love God," and hates his brother, he is a liar; for he who does not love his brother whom he has seen cannot love God whom he has not seen. 21 And this commandment we have from him: whoever loves God must also love his brother.* ESV

Q4. Why do you think 1 John primarily describes "love" from a negative perspective? What does 1 John say it means if we hate or do not love our brother?

Q5. Which verse or verses above are the most challenging for you? Why?

LOVE REQUIRES ACTION

In 1 John 3:11 the Apostle John says, "We should love one another." This is in response to the statement that love was the message they had heard from the beginning of their Christian experience when they had first heard the Gospel. Loving one another is also the subject of the last half of Chapter 3 of John's first epistle. He indicates to his audience what agape love is all about:

> **1 John 3:16-18** *By this we know love, that he laid down his life for us, and we ought to lay down our lives for the brothers. 17 But if anyone has the world's goods and sees his brother in need, yet closes his heart against him, how does God's love abide in him? 18 Little children, let us not love in word or talk but in deed and in truth.* ESV

Agape love is not about what we "feel" about someone. Love demands action and that is confirmed in 3:18. The ultimate act of love would be "*that he lay down his life for his friends.*" (John 15:13)

Q6. Assuming the extreme act of laying down your life is not demanded of you, what kind of other activities might you engage in that would demonstrate your love for one another?

Make a list of some ways in which we can demonstrate love to one another:

1.

2.

3.

4.

THE NEEDS OF OTHERS

Agape love can be thought of like taking a hot apple pie to my neighbor just because I want to. And that is great, but I don't think that is the primary focus for the love God really wants us to demonstrate. He wants us to help meet the real needs of the one on the receiving end of our act of love. Being nice and kind is wonderful, but God wants us to get down in the trenches if necessary and meet the real needs of our neighbors, friends, and family.

This is a very important point that you do not want to miss. Acts of goodness and kindness are wonderful and are expected, if not required, from a Christ-follower. *Agape* love, however, is being the feet and hands of God. It is meeting real life needs. Identify in the following passages the real needs:

Mt 25:35-36 *For I was hungry and you gave me food, I was thirsty and you gave me drink, I was a stranger and you welcomed me, 36 I was naked and you clothed me, I was sick and you visited me, I was in prison and you came to me.* ESV

Romans 12:13 *Contribute to the needs of the saints and seek to show hospitality.* ESV

Acts 2:45 *And they were selling their possessions and belongings and distributing the proceeds to all, as any had need.* ESV

Heb 13:1, 3 *Let brotherly love continue. . . . 3 Remember those who are in prison, as though in prison with them, and those who are mistreated, since you also are in the body.* ESV

Q8. What does *agape* love demonstrate or accomplish?

1. For yourself:

2. For one loved:

3. For God:

4. To others:

When we are good and kind to our neighbor the one who most often gets the credit is self. But when we selflessly help someone in need, God often gets the credit. It is obvious that Scripture requires that we love our brothers. But how far should we take that love? What are the boundaries? We could give away all our money to the poor and helpless, but where do we stop?

Q9. What do the following passages tell us about why to love others?

2 Corinthians 9:12 2 Corinthians 9:12 *For the ministry of this service is not only supplying the _needs_ of the saints, but is also overflowing in many thanksgivings to God.* ESV

Titus 3:14 *And let our people learn to devote themselves to good works, so as to help cases of _urgent need_, and not be unfruitful.* ESV

Q10. What do you think Titus 3:14 above means?

LOVE YOUR NEIGHBOR AS YOURSELF

Matthew 22:37-40 *And he said to him, "_You shall love the Lord your God with all your heart and with all your soul and with all your mind_. 38 This is the great and first commandment. 39 And a second is like it: You shall love your neighbor as yourself. 40 On these two commandments depend all the Law and the Prophets."* ESV

Galatians 5:14 *For the whole law is fulfilled in one word: "You shall <u>love your neighbor as yourself</u>."* ESV

Think about what it means on a real and practical basis to love your neighbor as yourself.

Q11. For the following categories of people, list two things you could or might do that would qualify as agape love.

Family Member: (1) _____; (2) _____

Friend/Neighbor: (1) _____; (2) _____

Church Member: (1) _____; (2) _____

Stranger: (1) _____; (2) _____

Remember, agape means you meet another's <u>need</u> or help meet a <u>need</u> and do not expect anything in return. You are as concerned for the needs and problems of others as you are for your own. Their needs are on a par with your own. You don't necessarily put others first or ahead of your needs, but they are considered on an equal basis.

LOVE IS THE PROOF

Who are we? Are we disciples? Do our friends know or suspect we are Jesus followers? Why? *Agape* love is <u>the</u> distinguishing characteristic of a Jesus follower.

The Bible says that when we meet Jesus there will be those who say, "Lord, Lord, haven't we done wonderful things in your name?" And the Lord will say, "Depart from me. I never knew you" (see Matthew 7:22–23). What will determine if we are known by God? The answer relative to this study is that we have a right relationship with Christ. But "relationship" can be very hard to observe in some people so God says if you want to know if another is a brother or sister, look at their agape love. John 13:35 says we can identify Jesus disciples because they love one another.

Q12. So if you observe periodic random acts of love, is that evidence that one is a disciple?

In 1 Corinthians 13, Paul says that if man doesn't have love, then he is just a noisy brass or a clanging cymbal. Paul makes it very clear that we must have love above all other things. He says in 1 Corinthians 13:3 that even if we give all our wealth to the poor or lose our lives for the Kingdom, we have gained nothing if we do not have love. Wow!

Q13. What is the greater meaning of 1 Corinthians 13:3?

Paul says that love never fails and that love is greater than being able to prophesy (preach or teach), to have charismatic gifts, or to have a word of knowledge. Love must simply accompany all we do and say and when it doesn't, God is dishonored. In 1 Corinthians 8, Paul says knowledge can create pride and get someone all puffed up about himself, but love edifies or builds up.

Love for another taken to the extreme implies we would be willing to lay down our life for a brother, if needed (1 John 3:16). Paul does not go quite that far but in the Book of Romans he gives his view of love:

Romans 13:8-10 *Owe no one anything, except to love each other, for the <u>one who loves another has fulfilled the law</u>. 9 The commandments, "You shall not commit adultery, You shall not murder, You shall not steal, You shall not covet," and any other commandment, are summed up in this word: "<u>You shall love your neighbor as yourself.</u>" 10 Love does no wrong to a neighbor; therefore love is the fulfilling of the law.* ESV

We must really understand what Romans 13:8 says about love. First, it is an obligation, not merely a noble idea or a pleasant option. Second, it is first to God and then to our neighbor. And we are to do it just like we love ourselves. What does all this mean? It probably comes very close to meaning that anyone in my sphere of influence whose needs I am in a position to meet, God wants me to do so.

Q14. If all we did was love God and each other, would we fulfill the "law?"

John 13:35 *By this* [agape] *all will know that you are My disciples, if you have <u>love for one another</u>.*

Why is loving one another the definitive proof that one is a disciple? I think the answer to that question is because we cannot do it on our own. It requires the Spirit of God within us. We must be in Christ. We must be living in the Spirit. We must abide! And we can't do any of those things without being Jesus followers.

Q15. In the real world (in your life) what gets in the way of loving others?

PERSONAL REFLECTION

1. In your opinion what are the three most important characteristics of a person who successfully loves his neighbor?

2. What is the greatest example of love you have ever witnessed and how did you feel or react?

3. What is the key ingredient for you in making agape happen in your life?

SUMMARY

Scripture makes it quite clear that loving one another should not merely be an option for a Jesus follower.

John 15:9-14 *As the Father has loved me, so have I loved you. Abide in my love. 10 If you keep my commandments, you will abide in my love, just as I have kept my Father's* *commandments and abide in his love. 11 These things I have spoken to you, that my joy may be in you, and that your joy may be full. 12 This is my commandment, that you love one another as I have loved you. 13 Greater love has no one than this, that someone lays down his life for his friends. 14 You are my friends if you do what I command you. . . . 17 These things I command you, so that you will love one another.* ESV

We are commanded to love one another! Love is the ultimate gift in serving others. In 1 Corinthians 12:31, Paul says love is the "most excellent way." Paul also says in 1 Corinthians 13 that when it is all said and done there are three foundational attributes: faith, hope, and love. But he indicates that the most important one of these attributes is love. Paul further describes the importance and permanence of love in Colossians 3:14, and he uses a picture of a person getting dressed, and he says that you can choose anything you want but "put on love."

Colossians 3:14 *And above all these put on love, which binds everything together in perfect harmony.* ESV

Thus, we are to love one another. We are children of the living God. We have fellowship with God and with one another. We love our brothers and sisters, especially those in need. John describes this relationship characteristic in more graphic terms:

1 John 2:9-11 *Whoever says he is in the light and hates his brother is still in darkness. 10 Whoever loves his brother abides in the light, and in him there is no cause for stumbling. 11 But whoever hates his brother is in the darkness and walks in the darkness, and does not know where he is going, because the darkness has blinded his eyes.* ESV

It is not our responsibility to determine *why* someone needs our love. It is not our responsibility to determine *how* our love will be received. It is simply our responsibility to love and leave the rest to God.

Scripture makes it clear that loving God or one another should not be based on an evaluation of pros and cons. I am to love just as Jesus loved me. I am to do it just as if I were doing it for myself. This is a very high standard and therefore difficult to achieve because Satan, the world, and our flesh are all working against us.

As Jesus followers, we must put our trust in Christ, we must seek the power of the Holy Spirit, and we must enlist the help of others to accomplish the desired outcome.

Prayer
Lord, I need to show and demonstrate love to ___X___.
Please make that happen in my life.

My Prayer

What I Want to Remember

Enter some notes and information that you want to remember about this lesson. It might be a Scripture verse or two, something new you learned, something you want to do, something you want to change, or just something you want to be sure to remember.

Wisdom to Action
Challenge

How can you demonstrate Christ-like love to a fellow believer in a tangible way this week, especially someone you might find challenging to love?

Lesson 5
A Jesus Follower
SERVES ONE ANOTHER

For you were called to freedom, brothers.
Only do not use your freedom
as an opportunity for the flesh,
but through love serve one another.
Galatians 5:13 ESV

MEDITATION

Meditate on Galatians 6:2 during your Quiet Time this week.

Galatians 6:2 *Bear one another's burdens, and so fulfill the law of Christ.* ESV

Think about the following questions: (1) What are "burdens?" (2) Do I know the burdens of others? Why? Why not? (3) What does "the law of Christ" mean?

NOTES:

INTRODUCTION

John 13 is the first of five chapters where Jesus is preparing His disciples for the time when He will no longer be with them. Here we find the story of Jesus washing His disciple's feet. This act might be considered a form of cleansing and it prepares the disciples for Jesus telling them about the coming Holy Spirit. This event not only demonstrates Jesus' love for His disciples but puts His humility on display in spectacular fashion. Note that Judas was in the group when the feet were washed.

John 13:1-17

1 It was just before the Passover Feast. Jesus knew that the time had come for him to leave this world and go to the Father. Having loved his own who were in the world, he now showed them the full extent of his love.

2 The evening meal was being served, and the devil had already prompted Judas Iscariot, son of Simon, to betray Jesus.

3 Jesus knew that the Father had put all things under his power, and that he had come from God and was returning to God;

4 so he got up from the meal, took off his outer clothing, and wrapped a towel around his waist.

5 After that, he poured water into a basin and began to wash his disciples' feet, drying them with the towel that was wrapped around him.

6 He came to Simon Peter, who said to him, "Lord, are you going to wash my feet?"

7 Jesus replied, "You do not realize now what I am doing, but later you will understand."

8 "No," said Peter, "you shall never wash my feet." Jesus answered, "Unless I wash you, you have no part with me."

9 "Then, Lord," Simon Peter replied, "not just my feet but my hands and my head as well!"

10 Jesus answered, "A person who has had a bath needs only to wash his feet; his whole body is clean. And you are clean, though not every one of you."

11 For he knew who was going to betray him, and that was why he said not everyone was clean.

12 When he had finished washing their feet, he put on his clothes and returned to his place. "Do you understand what I have done for you?" he asked them.

13 "You call me 'Teacher' and 'Lord,' and rightly so, for that is what I am.
14 Now that I, your Lord and Teacher, have washed your feet, you also should wash one another's feet.
15 I have set you an example that you should do as I have done for you.
16 I tell you the truth, no servant is greater than his master, nor is a messenger greater than the one who sent him.
17 Now that you know these things, you will be blessed if you do them. NIV

In this passage Jesus continues talking about his leaving and tells the group about Judas. In Chapter 14 He says that, "I am the way," and promises to send the Holy Spirit. In Chapter 15 He describes the vineyard and says that He is the true vine. In Chapter 16 He describes the work of the Holy Spirit and then in Chapter 17 He prays for Himself, His disciples, and finally all believers. In Chapter 18 He is betrayed and arrested.

Q1. What is particularly meaningful to you about Jesus washing feet?

Q2. Why did Jesus wash the disciple's feet?

Q3. What is the promise in 13:17?

Q4. What is the principle being taught in the following verses?

Matthew 10:24 *A disciple is not above his teacher, nor a servant above his master.* ESV
Mark 10:45 *For even the Son of Man came not to be served but to serve, and to give his life as a ransom for many.* ESV

Q5. Whose feet is God calling you to wash by performing a timely or humble act of service?

1.

2.

SERVING ONE ANOTHER

The various Biblical words translated as "service" or "serving" in the New Testament have the following meanings:
- provide aid as a servant
- do ministry
- provide relief
- be a slave
- perform charitable functions

Paul says very clearly in Galatians 5:13 that we are to "serve one another." He further describes in 2 Corinthians another benefit of serving one another.

2 Corinthians 9:12 *For the ministry of this <u>service</u> is not only supplying the needs of the saints, but is also overflowing in many thanksgivings to God.* ESV

Q6. What is that benefit of serving?

Q7. Has this ever happened to you because of something you did as an act of service for someone?

The word "serve" in <u>our</u> language has many meanings in various contexts. The most appropriate meanings are related to serving one another:

- to furnish or supply something necessary
- to meet the needs of someone
- to supply help that benefits another

In reality, such actions could also be considered or thought of as loving one another.

There are many "one another" instructions in the New Testament. When we do something for "one another" we are serving that person in some way. We have listed below a number of instructions related to how we are to treat or interact with one another. Read through each of the following and try to get a sense of what God is saying to you through these instructions.

DEVOTED	Rom 12:10a	**Be devoted** to one another in brotherly love.
HONOR	Rom 12:10b	**Honor** one another above yourselves.
HARMONY	Rom 12:16	Live in **harmony** with one another.
JUDGMENT	Rom 14:13	Therefore let us **stop passing judgment**.

ACCEPTANCE	Rom 15:7	**Accept one another** . . .
UNITY	1 Cor 1:10	**Agree** with one another . . .
PATIENCE	Eph 4:2-3	**Be patient, bearing with one another** in love.
KINDNESS	Eph 4:32	Be **kind and compassionate** to one another.
CONFESS	James 5:16	Therefore, **confess your sins** to one another
PRAY		and **pray for one another.**
SUBMISSION	Eph 5:21	**Submit to one another** with reference for Christ.
TEACH	Col 3:16	**Teach and admonish** one another
ENCOURAGE	1 Thess 5:11	Therefore **encourage one another**
SPUR ON	Heb 10:24	**Spur one another** toward love and good deeds.
NOT SLANDER	James 4:11	Brothers, do **not slander** one another.
TRUTH	Eph 4:25	**Speak the truth**, each one to his neighbor.
HOSPITABLE	1 Peter 4:9	Offer **hospitality** without grumbling.
HUMILITY	1 Peter 5:5	All of you, clothe yourselves with **humility**.
LOVE	1 Peter 1:22	**Love one another** deeply, from the heart.
CONCERN	1 Cor 12:25	Have the same **concern** for each other.

Q8. What is your overall reaction to these "one another" verses listed above?

THE INTERESTS OF OTHERS

Philippians 2:1-4 *So if there is any encouragement in Christ, any comfort from love, any participation in the Spirit, any affection and sympathy, 2 complete my joy by being of the same mind, having the same love, being in full accord and of one mind. 3 Do nothing from rivalry or conceit, but in humility count others more significant than yourselves. 4 Let each of you look not only to his own interests, but also to <u>the interests of others</u>.* ESV

Q9. What does this mean to you? Write yourself a note telling yourself what application this passage has for you personally:
Note:

THE INTERESTS OF JESUS

1 Peter 4:10-11 *As each has received a gift, use it to serve one another, as good stewards of God's varied grace: 11 whoever speaks, as one who speaks oracles of God; whoever serves, as one who serves by the strength that God supplies—in order that in everything God may be glorified through Jesus Christ. To him belong glory and dominion forever and ever. Amen.* ESV

Q10. Are you fully using your gifts to serve one another? What specifically are you doing?

EXERCISE

Choose one of the "one another" passages above and make notes that you could share in your group to encourage others. Your notes might include:

(1) What does the instruction mean to <u>you</u>? [there are no wrong answers.]

(2) Does this come naturally for you or do you really have to work at it? <u>Why</u> is it easy or hard for you?

(3) Do you have suggestions to the group on how to do this or how to make it easier to do?

(4) Do you have a testimony you could share with the group concerning this instruction (good or bad)?

NOTES:

PERSONAL REFLECTION

1. List at least three ways you are currently serving:

THE CHURCH:

ONE ANOTHER:

2. Are you comfortable with the amount and quality of your service listed above? Why? Why not?

CONCLUSION

Ephesians 6:7 says that we are to serve wholeheartedly and that we should serve others as if we were serving the Lord. On several occasions Matthew says that if we want to be great we must be a servant. Serving others may get as close to the heart of God as anything we might do.

Jesus said He came to serve not to be served. Ephesians 2:10 says, that God also created us to do good works if we are Jesus followers. It seems clear that a Jesus follower is called to *serve*. We cannot be right with God and not serve one another.

Prayer
Lord, I want to serve. I want to be all you want me to be. Provide opportunities for me to serve and make sure I am alerted to these occasions.

My Prayer

What I Want to Remember

Enter some notes and information that you want to remember about this lesson. It might be a Scripture verse or two, something new you learned, something you want to do, something you want to change, or just something you want to be sure to remember.

Wisdom to Action
Challenge

What opportunity do you have this week to serve someone selflessly? How can you put their needs above your own in a practical way?

Lesson 6
Jesus Followers
SPEAK TRUTH to ONE ANOTHER

MEDITATION

Meditate on 2 Timothy 2:25-26 during your Quiet Time this week.

2 Timothy 2:25-26 . . . *correcting his opponents with gentleness. God may perhaps grant them repentance leading to a knowledge of the truth, 26 and they may escape from the snare of the devil, after being captured by him to do his will.* ESV

SPEAKING TRUTH

Speaking truth to someone can have several implications:

- Someone is confused, misinformed, or wrong about the meaning of Scripture, doctrine, or biblical teaching and we help them know and understand the truth of God's Word,

- Someone is committing sin and we "rebuke" them gently in love to help restore their relationship with Christ, or

- Someone is telling lies or taking liberties with the truth: lies, gossip, false witness, etc.

There are two sides to "speaking truth." The first is that we are the one speaking and attempting to help or correct another. The second is that we are the one on the receiving end of the truth. Neither of these situations is easy. Sin, lies, and biblical error are often overlooked or ignored. It often requires a special person to effectively confront another about sin and perhaps an even more special person to recognize and accept truth when they are confronted.

Proverbs 27:17 says, "As iron sharpens iron, so one man sharpens another." It is important that we have friends who will be honest and truthful with us. It is similar to the boss who does not want "yes men" surrounding him. A good boss wants people who will challenge his thinking and tell him when they think he is wrong.

EXHORTATION TO SPEAK TRUTHFULLY – IT DOES MATTER

Speaking truth biblically means exhortation, warning, or encouragement intended to direct persons in the correct behavior. Ephesians 4:25 says, "*Therefore, having put away falsehood, let each one of you speak the truth with his neighbor, for we are members one of another.*" ESV

Q1. What is the significance of the phrase, "we are members one of another?"

Q2. What do we learn from the following passages about being honest?

Proverbs 24:26 *Whoever gives an honest answer kisses the lips.* ESV
Proverbs 13:5-6 *The righteous hates falsehood, but the wicked brings shame and disgrace. 6 Righteousness guards him whose way is blameless, but sin overthrows the wicked.* ESV
Proverbs 14:25 *A truthful witness saves lives, but one who breathes out lies is deceitful.* ESV

Proverbs 11:1 *A false balance is an abomination to the Lord, but a just weight is his delight.* ESV
Proverbs 12:22 *Lying lips are an abomination to the Lord, but those who act faithfully are his delight.* ESV

Proverbs 13:11 *Wealth gained hastily will dwindle, but whoever gathers little by little will increase it.* ESV
Proverbs 19:9 *A false witness will not go unpunished, and he who breathes out lies will perish.* ESV

Proverbs 12:19 *Truthful lips endure forever, but a lying tongue is but for a moment.* ESV

Q3. What is the broader meaning of Proverbs 12:19?

CORRECTION

If somebody wanders away from the truth we are responsible for trying to restore that situation:

James 5:19-20 *My brothers, if anyone among you wanders from the truth and someone brings him back, 20 let him know that whoever brings back a sinner from his wandering will save his soul from death and will cover a multitude of sins.* ESV

Q4. What does it mean that "someone brings him back?"

Q5. In Galatians 6:1 Paul says those who are "spiritual" should talk to a brother caught in sin. Who is he talking about? Who is spiritual?
Galatians 6:1 *Brothers, if anyone is caught in any transgression, you who are spiritual should restore him in a spirit of gentleness. Keep watch on yourself, lest you too be tempted.* ESV

Q6. What does "restore" mean or imply in Galatians 6:1?

Q7. What does "in a spirit of gentleness" mean in Galatians 6:1?

Q8. What do we learn from the following passage?
Colossians 3:16 Let the word of Christ dwell in you richly, teaching and admonishing one another in all wisdom, singing psalms and hymns and spiritual songs, with thankfulness in your hearts to God. ESV

Q9. What specifically does Galatians 2:13 tell us?
Galatians 2:11-13 *But when Cephas came to Antioch, I opposed him to his face, because he stood condemned. 12 For before certain men came from James, he was eating with the Gentiles; but when they came he drew back and separated himself, fearing the circumcision party. 13 And the rest of the Jews acted hypocritically along with him, so that even Barnabas was led astray by their hypocrisy.* ESV

CONFRONTATION

We must be careful in confronting one another so that we do not damage relationships or create additional problems. Remember, someone who is sinning probably already knows it and they don't want someone openly confronting them with words of accusation, judgment, etc.

Q10. What advice does the Bible provide on confronting sin in the following passages?

Matthew 7:3, 5 *Why do you see the speck that is in your brother's eye, but do not notice the log that is in your own eye? . . . 5 You hypocrite, first take the log out of your own eye, and then you will see clearly to take the speck out of your brother's eye.* ESV

Colossians 3:16 *Let the word of Christ dwell in you richly, teaching and admonishing one another in all wisdom, singing psalms and hymns and spiritual songs, with thankfulness in your hearts to God.* ESV [See 2 Timothy 3:16]

Pausing and being patient is always a good alternative to quick reactions. Listen to God in prayer before you act!

Proverbs 27:6 *Faithful are the wounds of a friend; profuse are the kisses of an enemy.* ESV

Proverbs 9:8 *Do not reprove a scoffer, or he will hate you; reprove a wise man, and he will love you.* ESV

Proverbs 19:25 *Strike a scoffer, and the simple will learn prudence; reprove a man of understanding, and he will gain knowledge.* ESV

But there may be resistance. You or the one being corrected may respond in anger. Jeremiah 17:23 reports an example of this, "*Yet they did not listen or pay attention; they were stiff-necked and would not listen or respond to discipline.*" NIV

Q11. In your opinion, what should you do if you are rejected and ignored?

JUDGMENT

This study is directed primarily at believers, but it is important that we remember that the result of rejecting the truth of the Gospel is deadly for the unbeliever.

Romans 2:8-9 *but for those who are self-seeking and do not obey the truth, but obey unrighteousness, there will be <u>wrath and fury</u>. 9 There will be <u>tribulation and distress</u> for every human being who does evil, the Jew first and also the Greek.* ESV

2 Thessalonians 2:10-11 *and with all wicked deception for <u>those who are perishing</u>, because they refused to love the truth and so be saved. 11 Therefore God sends them a strong delusion, so that they may believe what is false.* ESV

Every person is going to have to decide sometime in their life whether the Gospel is true. Is Jesus who He says He is? It is extremely important that we get the answer correct because it is a matter of life and death!

PERSONAL REFLECTION

Do you have someone in your life, other than a spouse, to whom you could speak truth and who would speak the truth to you?

You should have both! It may be the same person, but we should have people (friends) in our life that "are closer than a brother." We need people who will listen when we need to talk and talk to us when we need to be corrected. If you do not have someone like this in your life – start looking. If you do, tell them how much you appreciate their friendship.

CONCLUSION

First and foremost our relationship with God must be right. If that relationship is not in alignment, then everything else in our life will be problematic in one way or another. If we are not honest with our spouse, family, friends, and co-workers, then our lives will likely be in chaos. Life could be filled with problems, disappointment, resentment, jealousy, and all kinds of drama.

The Book of Proverbs tells us again and again the importance of truth and honesty. It tells us of the problems that are created by lies and deception.

Urging and encouraging friends and fellow believers to conduct themselves worthy of Christ is the calling of all

Christians. It is more than just an appeal to morality. Eternal life may be hanging in the balance!

Prayer
Lord, help me to be truthful. Help me live my life in truth.

My Prayer

What I Want to Remember

Enter some notes and information that you want to remember about this lesson. It might be a Scripture verse or two, something new you learned, something you want to do, something you want to change, or just something you want to be sure to remember.

Wisdom to Action
Challenge

In what situation do you need to speak truth more boldly or live it out more authentically? What specific action can you take to align your words and actions with God's truth?

Lesson 7
A Jesus Follower
MAKES and TEACHES DISCIPLES

Go therefore and make disciples of all nations,
baptizing them in the name of the Father and
of the Son and of the Holy Spirit, teaching them to
observe all that I have commanded you. And behold,
I am with you always, to the end of the age.
Matthew 28:19-20 ESV

MEDITATION

Take time during this week and think about if you know someone who needs to be discipled. What do they need? How might you approach them? Who are they:

1.

2.

3.

Are you prepared to help one of these people? Do you want help in this responsibility? Who might assist you?

Part A – WHO IS A DISCIPLE?

So Jesus said to the Jews who had believed in him,
"If you abide in my word, you are truly my disciples."
John 8:31 ESV

DEFINITION

A disciple is a person growing in his or her relationship with Christ Jesus, who is eager to learn and apply the truth of the Word of God in his or her life, resulting in a deeper commitment to a Christ-like lifestyle and service.

In order to better understand this definition we will break it into its nine component parts:

1. A disciple is GROWING

Q1. What does it mean to be "growing"?

It is fair to conclude that if you are <u>not</u> growing in your faith, then you may not be a disciple! That does not mean you are not saved, but it does mean you may be stagnated in your faith.

> **Philippians 1:9** *And it is my prayer that your love may abound more and more, with knowledge and all discernment.* ESV

> **Ephesians 4:13** *We all attain to the unity of the faith and of the knowledge of the Son of God, to mature manhood, to the measure of the stature of the fullness of Christ.* ESV

Q2. How would you explain *"measure of the stature of the fullness of Christ"* in Eph 4:13?

2. A disciple has a RELATIONSHIP with Christ

We must understand that it's not about religion, it's about a personal relationship with Jesus. It's personal. It is not about holding a membership card or attending church. It's about following Jesus, being in the family of God, and being fully committed to Christ.

> **1 Corinthians 1:9** *God is faithful, by whom you were called into the fellowship of his Son, Jesus Christ our Lord.* ESV

> **John 17:3** *And this is eternal life, that they know you the only true God, and Jesus Christ whom you have sent.* ESV

3. A disciple is EAGER

Q3. What does being eager mean?

4. A disciple wants to LEARN

Q4. How do we learn?

5. A disciple will <u>APPLY</u> it in their life

1 Corinthians 16:14 *Let all that you do be done in love.* ESV

1 Peter 1:13 *Therefore, preparing your minds for action, and being sober-minded, set your hope fully on the grace that will be brought to you at the revelation of Jesus Christ.* ESV

Q5. What does it mean "to apply?"

6. A disciple will apply the <u>TRUTH</u> of the Word of God

James 1:25 *But the one who looks into the perfect law, the law of liberty, and perseveres, being no hearer who forgets but a doer who acts, he will be blessed in his doing.* ESV

Matthew 4:4 *But he answered, "It is written, Man shall not live by bread alone, but by every word that comes from the mouth of God."* ESV

Q6. What does applying the Word to your life mean?

7. A disciple makes a deeper <u>COMMITMENT</u>

Q7. What does deeper imply?

Q8. What does "commitment" mean to you?

8. A disciple works toward a <u>CHRIST-LIKE LIFESTYLE</u>

1 Thessalonians 2:12 *We exhorted each one of you and encouraged you and charged you to walk in a manner worthy of God, who calls you into his own kingdom and glory.* ESV

Q9. How would you describe a "Christ-like lifestyle?"

9. A disciple is committed to <u>SERVICE</u>

Galatians 5:13 *For you were called to freedom, brothers. Only do not use your freedom as an opportunity for the flesh, but through love serve one another.* ESV

1 Peter 4:10 *As each has received a gift, use it to serve one another, as good stewards of God's varied grace:* ESV

PART B – MAKING and TEACHING DISCIPLES

INTRODUCTION

Remember, we are talking about teaching individuals that are already in the family of God. We will address unbelievers and the Great Commission in Lesson 8.

TEACH ONE ANOTHER

2 Timothy 2:2 *and what you have heard from me in the presence of many witnesses entrust to faithful men who will be able to <u>teach</u> others also.* ESV

Romans 15:14 *I myself am satisfied about you, my brothers, that you yourselves are full of goodness, filled with all knowledge and able to <u>instruct</u> one another.* ESV

Colossians 3:16 *Let the word of Christ dwell in you richly, <u>teaching</u> and admonishing one another in all wisdom, singing psalms and hymns and spiritual songs, with thankfulness in your hearts to God.* ESV

THE GOAL

If we were to develop a "mission" statement describing what we are to do for new believers, it might look something like this:

1) <u>recruiting</u>: go to places they can be found
2) <u>educating</u>: teach them the foundational doctrines of the faith
3) <u>modeling</u>: exhibit the life of a Jesus follower
4) <u>teaching:</u> the goal is that they obey

Our hope should be to build a committed core of followers who will teach and inspire others. The Apostles learned and observed what Jesus was doing – He taught them by both word and deed. Therefore, we should do the same. One of the keys was that He spent time with them.

How did Jesus teach His disciples? What techniques did He employ with His disciples?

1) He taught them how to pray,
2) He used Scripture in His teaching and in confronting Satan's temptations,
3) He performed miracles and said if you don't believe what I say, then believe what I do,
4) He washed the disciples' feet, and
5) He delegated the work sending out the Twelve, as well as others, two by two.

EXAMPLE OF PAUL

1 Thessalonians 1:5-8 *because our gospel came to you not only in word, but also in power and in the Holy Spirit and with full conviction. You know what kind of men we proved to be among you for your sake. 6 And you became imitators of us and of the Lord, for you received the word in much affliction, with the joy of the Holy Spirit, 7 so that you became an example to all the believers in Macedonia and in Achaia. 8 For not only has the word of the Lord sounded forth from you in Macedonia and Achaia, but your faith in God has gone forth everywhere, so that we need not say anything.* ESV

Q10. What do Paul's words and actions say about discipleship? [Fill in the proper word]

1:5 we _____ among you

1:6 you became _____ of us

1:7 you became a _____ to all the believers

1:8 the Lord's _____ rang out

1:8 your _____ in God has become known everywhere

1 Thessalonians 2:6-12 *Nor did we seek glory from people, whether from you or from others, though we could have made demands as apostles of Christ. 7 But we were gentle among you, like a nursing mother taking care of her own children. 8 So, being affectionately desirous of you, we were ready to share with you not only the gospel of God but also our own selves, because you had become very dear to us. 9 For you remember, brothers, our labor and toil: we worked night and day, that we might not be a burden to any of you, while we proclaimed to you the gospel of God. 10 You are witnesses, and God also, how holy and righteous and blameless was our conduct toward you believers. 11 For you know how, like a father with his children, 12 we exhorted each one of you and encouraged you and charged you to walk in a manner worthy of God, who calls you into his own kingdom and glory.* ESV

Q11. Based on 1 Thessalonians 2 above, what do we learn about making disciples in the following verses?
2:7

2:8

2:9

2:10

2:11

2:12

Q12. How might you summarize what it means to "make disciples" based on the two passages from 1 Thessalonians above?

DISCIPLE-MAKING

Some may suggest that making disciples is the same as sharing your faith. But there is a real and important difference between sharing your faith or testimony and making disciples. The purpose of sharing your faith is to help convert unbelievers to believers. In making disciples, the individual is already a believer. Our intent is to build and encourage their faith so that they can stand firm against the doubts, trials, and temptations of life.

Remember our definition of a disciple: A disciple is a person growing in his or her _relationship_ with Christ Jesus, who is eager to _learn and apply_ the truth of the Word of God in his or her life, resulting in a deeper commitment to a _Christ-like lifestyle_ and service. Therefore, almost everyone needs to be discipled.

Certainly all new believers need someone who will invest time and effort in teaching them about the Bible and the Christian faith. Unfortunately, since the church often does such a poor job of this, there are many long-time believers who also need someone to invest in their lives so that they really understand what it means to have an intimate relationship with Christ.

Obviously believers will have different levels of growth and be at different points in their faith walk. New believers might be described as babies, then continuing with the family metaphor, we might have youth, adolescent, and adult believers. Their needs might be described as follows:

Category	Needs
BABY (new believer)	CHERISH (protection, love, knowledge)
CHILD (limited knowledge)	TEACH (strong consistent guidance)
ADOLESCENT (growing)	COACH (experience, responsibility)
ADULT (makes disciples)	MOTIVATE (leadership, self-discipline)

Following are some guidelines for investing in someone else's life in order to help them grow as a disciple:

1. Have a heart for God. If you don't, it will be obvious to the disciple.
2. Develop a heart for your disciple.
3. Live a godly life. 1 Corinthians 11:1 says, "Follow my example, as I follow the example of Christ." If you don't, you will have no credibility.
4. Be a real friend so that you can be trusted and talk about important issues.
5. Address the disciple's needs individually. Do not become locked into some programmed agenda.
6. Recognize that God is in charge.
7. Pray for the disciple.
8. Be patient. Go at a speed that is comfortable for the disciple. This isn't a race.
9. Be persistent. Don't get off track.
10. Don't push too hard. Too much pressure can cause the disciple to question your motives.
11. Encourage the disciple to (a) be in church, (b) be in a small group.
12. Discern the spiritual needs of the disciple. Listen carefully and observe words and behavior.
13. Be a humble servant to the disciple. Put their needs first.
14. Be open and honest.

15. Hold the disciple accountable for (a) assigned homework if needed, (b) observable sin, and (c) meeting regularly.
16. Be encouraging.
17. Consider the plans, goals, and objectives of the disciple. This will depend a lot on the maturity of the disciple.
18. Focus on the Bible. Other material will work, but the disciple needs to learn and understand the Bible.
19. Make the time together one of joy – don't take yourself too seriously!
20. Don't waste time with the uncommitted. If the individual is uncommitted you can't make a disciple. The focus for that person must be conversion and salvation, not disciple making.[2]

PERSONAL REFLECTION:

Q13. Is there some reason you could not disciple another believer?

Q14. Do you need to be discipled?

CONCLUSION

What is discipleship? It is teaching another believer about Christ. It is helping a friend and investing your time in their life. It is assisting them to live a Christian life. And, it is all for the glory of God. The Bible says that we are being conformed to the likeness of Christ and that's the ultimate goal of discipleship.

The process of discipleship may seem daunting – it shouldn't. We are simply asked to share with another so they grow spiritually in the knowledge of God such that their lifestyle begins to take on the characteristics of one who has a right relationship with God. A good place to start in this endeavor might be to read the fundamental book in this Series: "*The RELATIONSHIP CHARACTERISTICS of a Jesus Follower: Are you right with God?*"

If you are still unsure of what to do and how to do it, study 1 Thessalonians 2:1-12 in some detail and follow the instructions in that passage. Making a disciple is no more than sharing the truth of God's Word with another and then modeling that truth. Pass on what you know and if something is lacking, you can tackle the issue together.

It is everyone's responsibility to be involved with the discipleship process. We can all disciple others to some degree and to some extent. The real question is, "Are you willing?" If you are, begin praying that God would open a door and point you in the right direction. We can all help make disciples. We will not all do it in the same way, but Jesus wants us to do it. The Kingdom is at hand, the time is now, and we need to be ready!

Prayer

Lord, if there is someone you wish me to disciple, please bring it to my attention and give me your knowledge and strength to represent You in grace and truth.

My Prayer

What I Want to Remember

Enter some notes and information that you want to remember about this lesson. It might be a Scripture verse or two, something new you learned, something you want to do, something you want to change, or just something you want to be sure to remember.

Wisdom to Action
Challenge

Who in your life could benefit from intentional discipleship? What step can you take this week to invest in their spiritual growth?

Lesson 8
A Jesus Follower
SHARES JESUS with the WORLD

For God so loved the world, that he gave his only Son,
that whoever believes in him should not perish
but have eternal life. For God did not send his Son
into the world to condemn the world, but in order
that the world might be saved through him.
John 3:16-17 ESV

INTRODUCTION

The first seven lessons have all been about how Jesus followers are to treat or relate to each other in order to be in harmony with God's plan for His people. We can't be right with God and not be right with one another.

But being right with God also requires that we are right with the world – people who are not Jesus followers. We will address that subject in this lesson.

THE PRIORITY

Matthew 6:33 ESV *But seek first the kingdom of God and his righteousness, and all these things will be added to you.*

Matthew 13:44-46 *The kingdom of heaven is like treasure hidden in a field, which a man found and covered up. Then in his joy he goes and sells all that he has and buys that* *field. 45 Again, the kingdom of heaven is like a merchant in search of fine pearls, 46 who, on finding one pearl of great value, went and sold all that he had and bought it.* ESV

Jesus describes the Kingdom in Matthew 13 as priceless! Why? Because the Kingdom is eternal! It is the hope of glory. If we seek to prosper in His righteousness, He will supply all our needs ("all these things will be given to you"). What this means is that we should seek Him and His Kingdom before any other worldly objectives. He can supply all our needs in Christ Jesus!

Paul demonstrated his commitment to the lost and His obedience to Christ by preaching about the Kingdom:

Acts 19:8 *And he entered the synagogue and for three months spoke boldly, reasoning and persuading them about the kingdom of God.* ESV [also Acts 28:23, 31]

We should be seeking a right relationship with God, with one another, and with the world. These relationships work only if we have our priorities in order:

Hebrews 3:1 *Therefore, holy brothers, you who share in a heavenly calling, consider Jesus, the apostle and high priest of our confession,* ESV

The focus must be on Jesus! First and foremost we need a right relationship with God, characterized by an intimate, growing love relationship with Christ. If Jesus and the Kingdom are not the central focus, our lives and our faith walk can become ineffective and frustrating.

THE GREAT COMMISSION

Matthew 28:19-20 *Go therefore and make disciples of all nations, baptizing them in the name of the Father and of the Son and of the Holy Spirit, 20 teaching them to observe*

all that I have commanded you. And behold, I am with you always, to the end of the age. ESV

One question to consider is, "What are God's primary goals for the church age?" I am sure they would include:

1. Saving the lost (Jews and Gentiles).
2. Sanctifying the church (see 2 Peter 3).
3. Ultimately destroying evil.

Of these three goals Scripture tells us to be involved with saving the lost. We are given the Great Commission in Matthew 28:18ff.

As part of the Great Commission, He said to us, "And surely I am with you always, to the very end of the age." His yoke is easy and the burden is light, and He set the example. He said, "I have set you an example that you should do as I have done for you."

JESUS CHOSE TWELVE

Mark 3:14 *And he appointed twelve (whom he also named apostles) so that they might be with him and he might send them out to preach* ESV

Jesus' teaching and disciple making activities took several forms. He taught large crowds so there was a corporate form to His work. He formed a small group of twelve followers with whom He spent three years of His life. He often taught and corrected individual disciples in one-on-one situations. But the primary focus of Jesus' ministry was teaching the Apostles, because they were the ones who would carry on after He was gone.

Jesus selected three of the Twelve for special training: Peter, James, and John. We see these three alone with Jesus on special occasions (Transfiguration, in room with Jairus' daughter, etc.). Jesus did not ignore the masses, but only a few seemed to be converted when He spoke to large crowds. His goal was to train the Apostles so that they would go out and take the Gospel to the world.

Based on the first five words of Matthew 28:19, we all have the same goal: "Therefore go and make disciples."

DO IT NOW

John 9:1-5 *As he passed by, he saw a man blind from birth. 2 And his disciples asked him, "Rabbi, who sinned, this man or his parents, that he was born blind?" 3 Jesus answered, "It was not that this man sinned, or his parents, but that the works of God might be displayed in him. 4 We must work the works of him who sent me while it is day; night is coming, when no one can work. 5 As long as I am in the world, I am the light of the world." ESV*

The message for us is that the time is <u>now</u>. Time may be running out. There may not be time to pray for or share your testimony with someone at a later date. There are a number of reasons that urgency may be necessary:

1. you or the person may die;

2. you or they may move away and you will never see that person again;

3. that person's heart may become hardened by time or circumstance and the opportunity is lost; or

4. you may be God's plan for delivering the Gospel.

THE PLIGHT OF THE LOST

Philippians 3:18-19 . . . *I have often told you and now tell you even with tears, walk as enemies of the cross of Christ. 19 Their end is destruction, their god is their belly, and they glory in their shame, with minds set on earthly things.* ESV

2 Thessalonians 1:7-9 this will happen *when the Lord Jesus is revealed from heaven with his mighty angels 8 in flaming fire, inflicting vengeance on those who do not know God and on those who do not obey the gospel of our Lord Jesus. 9 They will suffer the punishment of eternal destruction, away from the presence of the Lord . . .* ESV

Hebrews 10:26-27 *For if we go on sinning deliberately after receiving the knowledge of the truth, there no longer remains a sacrifice for sins,27 but a fearful expectation of judgment, and a fury of fire that will consume the adversaries.* ESV (see also 2 Peter 2:4-10; Jude 5-7)

Revelation 20:15 *And if anyone's name was not found in the book of life, he was thrown into the lake of fire.* ESV

Q1. How would you summarize the plight of the lost as described above?

Do you believe these passages describe your unbelieving friends? Do you believe that there is a hell and unbelievers will be in everlasting torment? If you do not believe, then why do you believe in eternal life when you accepted Christ? The Scriptures seem very clear that the unbeliever's home is eternal torment and life with Christ is an eternal relationship – we are with Him forever.

Are you reluctant to believe in eternal hell because you don't like that idea or concept? But eternal truth is not based on whether you like it or not. The problem with choosing what you want to believe and not want to believe is that it is a downward spiral to apostasy.

THE HARVEST FIELDS

Matthew 9:37-38 *Then he said to his disciples, "The harvest is plentiful, but the laborers are few; 38 therefore pray earnestly to the Lord of the harvest to send out laborers into his harvest."* ESV (see also John 4:34-38)
1 Corinthians 3:6-8 *I planted, Apollos watered, but God gave the growth. 7 So neither he who plants nor he who waters is anything, but only God who gives the growth. 8 He who plants and he who waters are one, and each will receive his wages according to his labor.* ESV

Q2. What do these verses mean to you?

Q3. Do you think that Matthew 9:37-38 implies that praying is adequate or sufficient?

Q4. If you believe that your responsibility ends with prayer, then how do you explain Jesus sending out twelve in Matthew 10 and seventy-two in Luke 10?

THE SOWER AND THE REAPER

John 4:34-38 *Jesus said to them, "My food is to do the will of him who sent me and to accomplish his work. 35 Do you not say, 'There are yet four months, then comes the harvest'? Look, I tell you, lift up your eyes, and see that the fields are white for harvest. 36 Already the one who reaps is receiving wages and gathering fruit for eternal life, so that sower and reaper may rejoice together. 37 For here the saying holds true, 'One sows and another reaps.' 38 I sent you to reap that for which you did not labor. Others have labored, and you have entered into their labor." ESV*

Q5. Who or what is a sower?

Q6. Who or what is a reaper?

Q7. Do <u>you</u> perceive that the harvest is currently plentiful – that the fields are ripe? Why? Why not?

Q8. Do you think we are to be both sowers and reapers? Why? Why not?

STUMBLING BLOCKS

1 Corinthians 9:19-23 *For though I am free from all, I have made myself a servant to all, that I might win more of them. 20 To the Jews I became as a Jew, in order to win Jews. To those under the law I became as one under the law (though not being myself under the law) that I might win those under the law. 21 To those outside the law I became as one outside the law (not being outside the law of God but under the law of Christ) that I might win those outside the law. 22 To the weak I became weak, that I might win the weak. I have become all things to all people, that by all means I might save some. 23 I do it all for the sake of the gospel, that I may share with them in its blessings.* ESV

Q9. Explain the above passage.

God tells us not to put stumbling blocks in the path of unbelievers that would cause them not to believe:

1 Corinthians 10:31-33 *So, whether you eat or drink, or whatever you do, do all to the glory of God. 32 Give no offense to Jews or to Greeks or to the church of God, 33 just as I try to please everyone in everything I do, not seeking my own advantage, but that of many, that they may be saved.* ESV

Q10. In the following passages, what occurred so that there would be no stumbling block?

Acts 16:3 *Paul wanted Timothy to accompany him, and he took him and circumcised him because of the Jews who were in those places, for they all knew that his father was a Greek.* ESV

Acts 18:18 *After this, Paul stayed many days longer and then took leave of the brothers and set sail for Syria, and with him Priscilla and Aquila. At Cenchreae he had cut his hair, for he was under a vow.* ESV

Acts 21:21-26 *". . . and they have been told about you that you teach all the Jews who are among the Gentiles to forsake Moses, telling them not to circumcise their children or walk according to our customs. 22 What then is to be done? They will certainly hear that you have come. 23 Do therefore what we tell you. We have four men who are under a vow; 24 take these men and purify yourself along with them and pay their expenses, so that they may shave their heads. Thus all will know that there is nothing in what they have been told about you, but that you yourself also live in observance of the law. 25 But as for the Gentiles who have believed, we have sent a letter with our judgment that they should abstain from what has been* *sacrificed to idols, and from blood, and from what has been strangled, and from sexual immorality." 26 Then Paul took the men, and the next day he purified himself along with them and went into the temple, giving notice when the days of purification would be fulfilled and the offering presented for each one of them.* ESV

Paul deprived himself of certain "rights" in order that others would listen and accept him and his message. He conformed his practices to the Jewish law, although he did not need to. He accommodated the Gentile culture when it did not violate his faith in order to reach non-Jewish unbelievers. He did not always exercise his Christian rights in order not to upset the people to whom he was talking. He did this in order to share in the blessing of seeing others come to Christ.

Q11. So, how far should we go in entering the "unbelievers" culture? What can we do? What shouldn't we do?

Q12. What do you think is the biggest hurdle in talking to someone about God and Jesus?

Choose one of the following reasons and explain why it is a hurdle: (1) raising the subject; (2) explaining the Gospel; (3) answering questions; (4) bringing them to decision point; (5) introducing the "sinner's prayer."

Your Explanation:

PRAYER

Colossians 4:2-4 *Continue steadfastly in prayer, being watchful in it with thanksgiving. 3 At the same time, pray also for us, that God may open to us a door for the word, to declare the mystery of Christ, on account of which I am in prison— 4 that I may make it clear, which is how I ought to speak.* ESV

Paul requests prayer that he might proclaim Christ. We should pray diligently for those with a gift of evangelism. Who do you know locally or in the mission field that needs the kind of prayer described by Paul in Colossians 4:2-4? List those names below:

1.

2.

3.

We should also pray diligently for those who are lost, particularly members of our family, friends, neighbors, and co-workers. Who are you (or should you be) praying for to receive Christ? List their names below:

1.

2.

3.

Prayer for the Lost: Lord, I pray that You will send a messenger, a harvest worker, to ___X___ to proclaim the Gospel. Allow ___X___ to know the truth – that Jesus is their Redeemer, Lord, and the Son of God. Convict them of sin and reveal to them that Jesus has paid that sin debt. Give them the courage necessary to ask Christ into their heart. Lord give ___X___ life everlasting.

What I Want to Remember

Enter some notes and information that you want to remember about this lesson. It might be a Scripture verse or two, something new you learned, something you want to do, something you want to change, or just something you want to be sure to remember.

Wisdom to Action
Challenge

Consider your daily interactions. With whom can you share the Gospel this week? How can you prepare yourself to seize this opportunity to be a witness?

Exhibit A
Groups that need to hear the gospel?

Chose one of these groups (or select one not listed) and write out a response to the following questions for the group you select:

Q. What barriers exist between us and the group?

Q. What do we have in common?

Q. What rights must we give up in order to relate to this group?

Q. What special needs does this group have that we could supply?

Q. How might we try to approach this group in order to ultimately share the Gospel?

	What Barriers	What in Common	Rights Give up
Poor/needy			
Addicted-drugs			
Addict-alcohol			
Sexual Predator			
Aged-Nursing Home			
Aged-Homebound			
Apathetic			

Rich			
Troubled Teens			
Youth			
HIV/Aids			
Sick			
Cult Members			
Foreigners			
Welfare			
Disabled			
Homeless			
Out-of-Work			

NOTES:

Lesson 9
A Jesus Follower is Called to a High Standard

"The most important thing is, whatever you do
decide to do, take it seriously
and do your best."
Tom Sturridge

"Act as if what you do makes a difference. It does."
William James

INTRODUCTION

This lesson is going to be different from the preceding 8 lessons in this study. We will examine the broader nature of what we are called to do or be as Jesus-followers and the nature of that calling.

Regardless of what you exactly believe the Lord requires of you, based on this study, you must sense by now that believers are called to a very high standard of conduct and commitment. That ultimate standard is defined by Christ because the Bible says that we are being transformed into the likeness of Christ. God wants to transform us into the likeness of His Son.

2 Corinthians 3:18 *And we, who with unveiled faces all reflect the Lord's glory, are being <u>transformed</u> into his likeness with ever-increasing glory, which comes from the Lord, who is the Spirit.*
[see also Romans 8:29-30]

Ultimately, the standard is perfection:

Ephesians 1:4 *For he chose us in him before the creation of the world to be <u>holy and blameless</u> in his sight.* [See also Eph 5:25-28; Phil 1:9-11, 2:14-15]

Matthew 5:48 *<u>Be perfect</u>, therefore, as your heavenly Father is perfect.* [See also Colossians 1:28]

These Scriptures alone might be enough to convince you of the very high calling God has put on the lives of Jesus-followers. The question you may have is, "What level of obedience or relationship is God *really* looking for?"

There are many specific instructions or commands in the Bible that suggest the standard is very high. For example:

1) Holiness (be holy as I am holy)
1 Peter 1:14-16 *As obedient children, do not be conformed to the passions of your former ignorance, 15 but as he who called you is holy, you also be holy in all your conduct, 16 since it is written, "<u>You shall be holy, for I am holy</u>."* ESV

2) Imitate Christ
Ephesians 5:1-2 *Therefore <u>be imitators of God,</u> as beloved children. 2 And walk in love, as Christ loved us . . .* ESV

3) Obedience
1 John 2:3-4 *And by this we know that we have come to know him, <u>if we keep his commandments</u>. 4 Whoever says*

"I know him" but does not keep his commandments is a liar, and the truth is not in him, ESV

4) Kind, Compassionate, and Forgiving
Ephesians 4:32 *Be <u>kind</u> to one another, <u>tenderhearted</u>, forgiving one another, as God in Christ forgave you.* ESV

5) Goodness
Job 1:8 . . ."*Have you considered my servant Job, that there is none like him on the earth, a <u>blameless</u> and <u>upright</u> man, who fears God and <u>turns away from evil</u>?*" ESV

6) Justice
Isaiah 56:1 *Be <u>just</u> and <u>fair</u> to all, says the LORD. Do what is <u>right</u> and <u>good</u>* . . . NLT

7) Love
1 John 4:8 *Anyone who <u>does not love does not know God</u>, because God is love.* ESV

8) Submission
James 4:7 <u>Submit yourselves therefore to God</u>. . . . ESV

9) Compassion, Kindness, Humility, Gentleness, Patience,
Colossians 3:12 Put on then, as God's chosen ones, holy and beloved, <u>compassion, kindness, humility, meekness, and patience,</u> ESV

You might respond to these passages by saying, "It's hopeless. There is no way I can live up to these standards!" In reality, we cannot. It is only those who have truly been saved and have the power of God living within them that can consistently achieve what God desires. These verses confirm that there are very high expectations for the true disciple. Frankly, why shouldn't there be? Since we are being conformed to the image of Christ – what other expectation can there be?

There are many other passages throughout Scripture that tell us how to act or give us instruction about what God expects from us. These Scriptures surely lead one to think that the conditions identified are real and not just warnings to "scare" us into obedience.

A CONDITIONAL LIFESTYLE

Life on this side of heaven is a series of decisions and those choices determine much about the nature and success of our earthly lives. For example, we make very important choices when we pick our college, our spouse, our church, whether we will have children, where we will live, what jobs we will accept, etc. In most of these choices we do not know the ultimate outcome of that decision, but in the Bible the result of many decisions is foretold. The most obvious is that if we accept Jesus as our personal savior we receive eternal life.

Many of the conditional promises in the Bible are about our lifestyle. Secular decisions depend on our ability to understand the choices we face and then make a "good" decision. But in the Bible for many situations we know the promised result in advance. This conditional lifestyle did not begin with Christ. Adam and Eve were told that they were not to eat from the tree of the knowledge of good and evil and *if* they did they would surely die. They had a choice and they knew the result and the consequence.

Abraham received a conditional covenant or pledge that God would be His God and the God of His descendants *if* the people would be totally consecrated to the Lord. Israel was given the Law (Old Covenant) and they were told what would happen if they did not keep the law (Ex 19-24; Dt 11:26ff). After Israel sinned and continued to rebel against God, He sent the prophets to warn the people of the coming judgment (exile) that awaited them *if* they did not choose to repent. Israel ignored the warnings of the prophets and the destruction of the people, temple and lands occurred just as God warned them.

Many of the promises in the Bible are conditional in nature. Therefore, we need to understand what God is asking of us. I don't really need to understand the underlying purpose of God's promises; I just need to understand and believe that when God says that *if* I do something, the result He promises will occur. I am fully aware of what the benefits or consequences (good and bad) will be, so I can make good choices.

For example, Matthew 10:32 says, "*Whoever acknowledges me before men, I will also acknowledge him before my Father in heaven.*" (HCSB) The skeptic may point out that this does not say that the Father will not acknowledge us. True, but what sane person would want to take that chance? Matthew 6:14-15 covers both sides of the issue:

> *For if you forgive others their trespasses, your heavenly Father will also forgive you, 15 but if you do not forgive others their trespasses, neither will your Father forgive your trespasses.* ESV

The importance of these conditions is that Scripture gives us clear guidelines for a healthy and satisfying life – it points us toward the positive side of a Christian lifestyle. If we positively respond to these conditions and promises, we will receive the promised benefits. For example Romans 8:28 says that God will work in my life, but only for those "who love Him." See other examples in Luke 6:38; Philippians 4:6-7; and 1 Peter 5:6.

"SO THAT" CONDITIONAL PROMISES

You may be prepared to grant the idea that our lives are influenced by the choices we make. But you may not be aware of the extent the Bible tells us about what we should do and what the consequences will be.

In order to illustrate this point we will look at two small words that occur often throughout Scripture: "so that." In the NIV translation this phrase occurs a total of 744 times, 291 times in the New Testament. A closer examination of these occurrences reveals that most of these fall into two categories:

- things Jesus or God has done for us "so that" something will happen, and

- things we should do "so that" we receive some benefit or avoid something negative.

For this purpose we will look only at the passages that deal with how we are to act and the resulting benefit of that action. First, let's examine the four Gospels and what Jesus Himself has to say.

JESUS – Teaching to disciples and crowds

Jesus makes a number of "so that" statements in the Gospels:

Verse	Do this	So that this happens or is the result
Matt 6:3-4	give to the needy	give in secret
Matt 6:17-18	fast	fasting is not obvious
Matt 26:41	watch and pray	not fall into temptation
Mark 11:24-25	forgive	God the Father will forgive us
Luke 16:8-9	use wealth to gain friends	welcome in heaven
John 12:36	put trust in the light	may become sons of light
John 14:13-14	ask (pray) in my name	(a) Son bring glory to Father

		(b) it will be given
John 15:2	expect to be pruned	bear more fruit
John 15:10-11	obey	my joy may be complete
John 16:1	understand/listen to Word	you will not go astray
John 16:33	understand/listen to Word	you have peace

You might expect Jesus to make such statements but you may not be aware how frequently a conditional lifestyle is described throughout the remainder of the Bible. There are numerous Scriptures that describe the conditional nature of our relationship to God. He clearly tells us in His Word what He wants to do in our lives. We have summarized His instructions into two groups as follows:

Instructions: (what we should do)

Jesus tells us in the Gospels to: give to the needy, fast, watch and pray, forgive, use our wealth wisely, put trust in the light, obey, and understand and listen to the Word. Then there are additional groups of "so that" passages that we have grouped into eleven categories that focus on a particular subject. We have not provided all the Scripture references and detail because of space constraints.

1. SIN: Repent and turn to God
2. EVANGELISM: Proclaim the Gospel
3. GLORIFY GOD: In all things God should be praised
4. UNITY: There should be unity in the church
5. BOASTING: We must not boast, unless about God
6. POWER: We should seek God's power in our lives
7. RIGHTEOUSNESS: We are called to live rightly before God
8. SUFFERING: Endure it – it's bound to happen
9. KNOW GOD: Woe is me if Christ says, "I don't know you"
10. KNOWLEDGE: Know the Word to make good choices
11. PERSEVERE: Persevere and not give up

Blessings: (what we will receive if we obey)

If we obey Jesus He said we would: know that God the Father will forgive us, be welcome in heaven, become sons of light, bear fruit, not go astray, and have peace. These alone might seem enough but there is much more to receive if we obey God's many other conditional promises:

- Our sins are wiped out or forgiven and we are not hardened by sin's deceitfulness.
- We can experience the joy of proclaiming the truth and knowing unbelievers are saved.
- God is praised, worshipped, and glorified.
- There is no division in the church – we are united.
- We are able to boast about the Lord, the church, or our weakness – giving God the credit.
- We have great faith, endurance and patience.
- We are blameless.
- We comfort others.
- We can be generous on every occasion.
- We are able to lead a quiet life.
- We can rejoice, even in trials.
- We can discern what is best and be pure and blameless, filled with the fruit of righteousness.
- We can encourage others and rebuke those in error.
- We do not drift away or be carried away by error.
- We have assurance of our salvation and become mature in our faith.

These blessings are achieved only through our obedience! They become reality if I obey the particular condition "*so that*" I receive the promised result. One might say, "Why wouldn't we want all these blessings in our life? Why does sin and rebellion win so often? Why are so many people living in bondage and not intentionally seeking the blessings of God's promises?"

The answer can only be ignorance, apathy, unbelief, or rebellion. The cause might be Satan, the evil in this world, or the sinful nature within us that we have not yet conquered.

FREEDOM IN CHRIST

Someone might suggest that there is "freedom" in Christ and thus there are no rules we _must_ obey. That raises the question of whether we are free to live our lives as we please or are we living our lives as slaves to a set of rules and laws? Do we have freedom in Christ or not? What does "freedom in Christ" really mean?

Galatians 5:1 says, "_It is for freedom that Christ has set us free. Stand firm, then, and do not let yourselves be burdened again by a yoke of slavery_." (NIV) In Ephesians 3:12 Paul says that "_we may approach God with freedom and confidence._" And, in John 8, the Bible says, "_you will know the truth, and the truth will set you free_ . . . _So if the Son sets you free, you will be free indeed._" (NIV)

The Bible seems very clear about our freedom. We can find other verses that say or directly imply that we are no longer slaves to the law. In other words, there is not a list of requirements that must be followed for us to be saved because we do not _earn_ our salvation.

But then what is this "freedom" we have in Christ? Are we free to do anything we want or are we restricted in some way? What does Scripture say about how we should conduct our lives in this freedom and what are the implications? Corinthians 8:9 tells us pretty directly that we must "_Be careful, however, that the exercise of your freedom does not become a stumbling block to the weak._" And, Corinthians 10:31-32 also makes it very clear: "_So whether you eat or drink or whatever you do, do it all for the glory of God. Do not cause anyone to stumble, whether Jews, Greeks or the church of God._" Corinthians 10:23

says, "*Everything is permissible – but not everything is beneficial. Everything is permissible – but not everything is constructive. Nobody should seek his own good, but the good of others.*"

Even though we are "free," that freedom should not be exercised in such a way that others could be negatively impacted or God dishonored. The various translations describe this concept as freedom, a right, or as liberty

The Bible further tells us about how our freedom in Christ should impact our own lives:

> **Galatians 5:1** *For freedom Christ has set us free; stand firm therefore, and do not submit again to a yoke of slavery.* ESV

> **Galatians 5:13-15** *For you were called to freedom, brothers. Only do not use your freedom as an opportunity for the flesh, but through love serve one another. 14 For the whole law is fulfilled in one word: "You shall love your neighbor as yourself."15 But if you bite and devour one another, watch out that you are not consumed by one another.* ESV

> **1 Peter 2:16-17** *Live as people who are free, not using your freedom as a cover-up for evil, but living as servants of God. 17 Honor everyone. Love the brotherhood. Fear God. Honor the emperor.* ESV

In Romans 6:22, Paul says, "*But now that you have been set free from sin and have become slaves to God, the benefit you reap leads to holiness, and the result is eternal life.*" NIV

Yes, we are free in Christ, but that freedom comes with responsibilities. Freedom in Christ does not mean we can do anything we want without consequence. It means we are not under the Law to gain our <u>salvation</u>, but within that freedom we are called to a relationship with Christ that inherently demands a standard of performance that would honor Christ and glorify God.

CONCLUSION

The question is, "What is the nature of our calling? What does the Lord <u>really</u> require of us?" After reading this chapter you might want to suggest that the real question should be, "God can't be requiring all this, can He?"

What can we reasonably conclude from this seemingly overwhelming list of conditional promises? Does anybody actually live a lifestyle that seems to be required? Clearly God has an extremely high expectation for the church. The standard is set very high!

The key to achieving that high standard is a right relationship with God, with believers, and with the world. If the relationships are right we can live in peace, staking claim to the promises contained in God's Word. We know that the underlying core issue is man's problem with sin. We must find some way to solve our rebellion problem and our inherent sinful nature or we will be eternally estranged from God. The answer to that dilemma is Jesus!

The Bible is filled with promises of the abundant life if we obey the conditions set out in Scripture. Unfortunately, many believe we are entitled to the abundant life without conforming to God's requirements. Those who choose to ignore God's instructions and commands are living in rebellion. The result of that type of lifestyle is usually misery and frustration. But, remember:

Hebrews 4:16 *Let us then with confidence draw near to the throne of grace, that we may receive mercy and find grace to help in time of need.* ESV

We have only touched the surface of what the Bible asks of us. In Appendix A, we have summarized the "holy living" requirements from four of the letters written by Paul. The task may seem overwhelming or even impossible. But nothing is impossible with God.

One conclusion we can clearly draw from this review of Scripture is that Christian living is not about doing it our way but about doing it God's way. The consequences of not doing it God's way are likely much greater than you and I want to believe.

One could try to list all the requirements and conditions in Scripture and then set goals to achieve all that but the following passage from Romans 12:1-2 may direct us in a more perfect path:

> *I appeal to you therefore, brothers, by the mercies of God, to present your bodies as a living sacrifice, holy and acceptable to God, which is your spiritual worship. 2 Do not be conformed to this world, but be <u>transformed by the renewal of your mind</u>, that by testing you may discern what is the will of God, what is good and acceptable and perfect.* ESV

He wants our entire life and He wants to transform us into the likeness of Christ. We must no longer be driven by the values of this world, but be changed and transformed by the renewing of our minds by the Word of God. Our responsibility is to pursue an intimate relationship with Him so that He can work through us to achieve His purpose for us.

DISCUSSION QUESTIONS

1. In 2 Corinthians 3:18 and Romans 8:29-30 we're told we are being transformed and conformed into the likeness of Christ. How do you think that is happening? What do you think that means? Explain.

2. Do you think God absolutely requires the type of lifestyle described in this lesson? Or, is it only His hope for us? Why? Why not?

3. How would you demonstrate or prove to an unbeliever that you love God?

4. In Micah 6:8 the people were told to, "walk humbly with your God." What do you think that means?

5. Matthew 6:14-15 says *"For if you forgive others their trespasses, your heavenly Father will also forgive you, 15 but if you do not forgive others their trespasses, neither will your Father forgive your trespasses.* ESV

Do you believe this is literally true? Why? Why not?

6. What do you think Paul means in Romans 6:22 when he says we have "become slaves to God?" Does he mean we have traded one slave master for another?

7. In the "so that" statements associated with Jesus, are there any conditions which you could not meet? Which one(s) would you find the most difficult? Why?

8. Do you think that the appeal for unity in the following verse is humanly possible?
1 Corinthians 1:10 *I appeal to you, brothers, by the name of our Lord Jesus Christ, that all of you agree and that there be no divisions among you, but that you be united in the same mind and the same judgment.* ESV

What I Want to Remember

Enter some notes and information that you want to remember about this lesson. It might be a Scripture verse or two, something new you learned, something you want to do, something you want to change, or just something you want to be sure to remember.

Wisdom to Action
Challenge

In what area of your life are you falling short of the high standard Christ calls us to? What specific change can you make this week to better reflect Christ's character in this area?

Appendix A
Rules for Christian living

(Col 3:1-17, 4:2-6; Eph 4 and 5; Ro 12:4-13:14; and 1 Thes 4; 5:12-22) *

WHY: Since we have been buried and raised with Christ we want to please God.

FOCUS: Set your heart and mind on spiritual things; imitate God; and understand God's will. Clothe yourself with the Lord Jesus Christ.

<u>Christ-like character:</u>
Galatians 5:22-23 *But the fruit of the Spirit is love, joy, peace, patience, kindness, goodness, faithfulness, gentleness and self-control.*

Love:	Love one another and others as yourself.
Righteousness:	Be compassionate, kind, gentle, good, wise, hospitable; do what is right.
Forgive:	Forgive one another.
Peace:	Live at peace with everyone.
Truth:	Speak truthfully in love; do not lie.
Patience:	Be patient in your afflictions and trials.
Humility:	Be humble; honor others above yourself; do not be proud.
Joyful:	Be joyful.

<u>Avoid Sin:</u>
Galatians 5:19-21 *The acts of the sinful nature are obvious: sexual immorality, impurity and debauchery; idolatry and witchcraft; hatred, discord, jealousy, fits of rage, selfish ambition, dissensions, factions and envy; drunkenness, orgies, and the like . . .*

Change:	Put off your old self and put on the new.
Anger:	Get rid of bitterness, rage, and anger; brawling, slander, and malice.
Sexual immorality:	Avoid sexual immorality, impurity, lust, and evil desires.

Evil:	Avoid evil, and overcome evil with good
Drunkenness:	Do not get drunk on wine
Work:	Do not steal, but work – do something useful, don't be idle.
Speech:	Do not let unwholesome talk come from your mouth; put off obscenity, foolish talk, coarse joking, slander, and filthy language – do not curse.

Act and Serve:

Galatians 5:6b, 14, . . . *The only thing that counts is faith expressing itself through love . . . 14 The entire law is summed up in a single command: "Love your neighbor as yourself."* . . .

Opportunities:	Make the most of every opportunity.
Knowledge:	Know what you are talking about; seek maturity in your faith.
Thanksgiving:	Give thanks to God in all circumstances for everything.
Sing (worship):	Speak to each other and God with Psalms, hymns, and spiritual songs.
Prayer:	Devote yourselves and be faithful in prayer.
the Needy:	Share with those in need.
Enemies:	Bless those who persecute you; give food and drink to your enemies.
Debt:	Give everyone what you owe them.
Strangers:	Be wise in the way you treat outsiders.
Leaders:	Respect your pastors – hold them in high regard; be careful of false teachers.
Unity:	Build up the church to reach unity in the faith.

*This is a summary of all the requirements for holy living outlined in these passages. There are many duplications in all these passages. We have combined, summarized, and categorized them here to make it easier to understand.

Transformation Road Map

Primary Takeaways

1: Consistent and intentional encouragement is a vital aspect of Christian community, serving to strengthen faith, prevent spiritual hardening, and promote unity among believers. Mutual encouragement is rooted in prayer and essential for spiritual growth and resilience in the face of life's challenges and the deceitfulness of sin.

2: Forgiveness is a divine command that reflects God's mercy, restores relationships, and frees believers from the spiritual and emotional bondage of bitterness. By forgiving others we experience peace and healing in our own lives.

3: Bearing fruit is expected of believers and comes from abiding in Christ. Disciples will produce good fruit (such as love, joy, peace, and other virtues) as a result of their intimate relationship with Him, rather than through our own efforts and strength.

4: Love for fellow believers is a defining characteristic and commandment for Jesus' disciples. This love serves as a powerful testimony to the world, demonstrating the authenticity of one's faith and relationship with Christ.

5: Serving one another is an expression of Christ-like love and humility. Jesus set the example by washing His disciples' feet, teaching that true discipleship involves selflessly meeting the needs of others.

6: Speaking truth to one another is essential for living out God's truth in our daily lives. Walking in truth involves not only speaking honestly but also aligning one's actions with God's Word.

7: Discipleship involves intentionally investing in the spiritual growth of other believers by teaching and modeling Christ-like behavior.

8: Being a witness to the world is a fundamental responsibility and urgent priority for all believers. Jesus followers are called to actively participate in the Great Commission by sharing the Gospel, making disciples, and demonstrating Christ's love to the lost.

9: A Jesus follower is called to a high standard because we are expected to live in holiness, integrity, and obedience, reflecting Christ's character in every aspect of our lives. This elevated standard is achievable only through a true relationship with God, empowered by His Spirit.

What are you being called to do next?

Leader Guide

This Guide is designed to give a leader answers and additional information to effectively lead a discussion of each lesson.

Tips For Leading

We recommend that you begin a group discussion by reading an appropriate Scripture. It may be one that you will cover in the material or another related passage you have chosen. This will do several things:

- Allow time for everyone to get settled.
- Remind everyone of the subject and bring their minds to a common focus.
- Provide a transition from the previous activity.

Additional ice-breakers are usually not necessary, but if your group is new or members don't know each other well, you could have someone give their testimony/story at the beginning of each week. If you sense that the group needs additional focus before you begin with the discussion, conduct a short discussion about the themes of the lesson or ask about the meaning of a particular term associated with the lesson.

Goals

The discussion should center around the questions in the lesson. But remember that each person in your group has different goals and is at a different place in his or her Christian walk. Jesus may be an old friend to some but a new acquaintance to others. The dynamic of the group will vary depending on the nature of the participants.

Your goal as the Leader should be to foster understanding and familiarity with Scripture. For new believers or participants who are not comfortable with the Bible, your goal should be to help them get over that hurdle and begin to seek knowledge and understanding from the Bible.

More mature participants will probably dig deeper to find personal meaning and understanding. They may particularly desire to discuss application questions and issues.

Prayer
Unless you have an outstanding person of prayer in your group, you as the leader should wrap up your discussion time with prayer that specifically reflects the discussion and the themes, purpose, and focus of the lesson.

Answers

Lesson 1 A Jesus Follower ENCOURAGES One Another
PART A – PRAY FOR ONE ANOTHER
Q1.
His Disciples:
17:11   Protect them – by the power of your name.
17:15   Protect then – from the evil one.
17:17   Sanctify them – by the truth (your Word).
Future Believers:
17:21a   That all may be one – just as we (Father/Son) are one.
17:21b   May they be in us – so the world will believe.
17:23   Brought to complete unity – so the world would know the Father sent the Son, so they would know You loved them.
17:24a   Be with Me where I am.
17:24b   See My glory.
Q2.
Unity
Q3.
The expressed purpose of that unity is: *so that the world would know* Him who was sent by God. John 17:21 May they also be in us so that the world may believe that you have sent me.
Q4.
1:9   Be filled with knowledge of His will.
          Why: Col1:10 says: in order live life worthy of Lord and please Him.
1:10a   Bear fruit in every good work.
1:10b   Grow in knowledge of God.
1:11   Strengthened with all power - so may have endurance and patience.
1:12   Give thanks to Father.
Q5. n/a
Q6. n/a
Q7.
Heart and mind vs. flesh or inner self (the heart) that controls your words and actions.

Q8.
Power to grasp how wide and long and high and deep is the love of Christ, and to know this love that surpasses knowledge.
Q9.
RESULT: That they may be filled to the measure of all the fullness of God.
MEANING: Sanctification.
Q10.
NATURE: They are eternal.
DESCRIPTION: They revolve around fundamental truths.

PART B – ENCOURAGE ONE ANOTHER
Q1.
So not become hardened by sin.
Q2.
That we get so used to sin it seems natural or right; that sin does not bother our conscience any longer.
Q3.
1:16 He often refreshed me (while everyone else deserted me).
1:16 Not ashamed of my chains.
1:17 He searched hard until he found me (diligent).
1:18 May the Lord grant him mercy.
1:18 Many ways he helped me.
LEADER: You might ask, "When is the last time you encouraged someone? What did you do?"
Q4.
Ro 1:11-12
HOW: Impart (share) spiritual gifts.
WHY: Increase faith.
Romans 12:8 *if it is encouraging, let him encourage; if it is contributing to the needs of others, let him give generously; if it is leadership, let him govern diligently; if it is showing mercy, let him do it cheerfully.* NIV
We should use our spiritual gift of encouragement.
Titus 1:9
HOW: Teach.
WHY: (a) Communicate sound doctrine (b) refute false teaching.
1Corinthians 14:30-31 *And if a revelation comes to someone who is sitting down, the first speaker should stop. 31 For you can all prophesy in turn so that everyone may be instructed and encouraged.* NIV
Colossians 2:1-2a
HOW: Pray.
WHY: Be united in love.
Q5. n/a
Q6. n/a

Lesson 2 A Jesus Follower FORGIVES One Another

MEDITATATION
LEADER: You might ask your group, "If all we had in Scripture was Ps 32:1-2, would this make sense?"

There is nothing said in 32:1-2 about the actions of the offender. Yes, someone may be forgiven, but that does not mean they have gained any standing or trust. These two verses say nothing about repentance.

INTRODUCTION

NO – only God can forgive sin, since all sin by definition is against God. We are not forgiving "sin" but forgiving the hurt that the offense caused us. The offender must still seek forgiveness from God for the sin.

LEADER: You might ask if your group thinks forgiving means:

We forget. Ans: No

We now trust that person. Ans: No

We let go of bitterness and desire for revenge. Ans: Yes

We rebuild trust only over time. Ans: Yes

Q1. n/a

Q2.

Ans: They likely want to punish the offender.

Q3.

Because Jesus forgave me, and because we are commanded to do so.

Q4.

Absolutely – if you don't think so, then you probably have a mis-understanding of your own inherent sinfulness.

Q5.

Harboring un-forgiveness is going to hurt us and be detrimental to our lives. The command is more for us and to benefit our ongoing lives, not to relieve the offender.

Q6.

Matthew 6:14-15 God will not forgive us if we do not forgive. God expects a forgiving spirit because He forgave us.

Mark 11:25-26 Conditional? We are to forgive, so the Father will forgive us. We need His forgiveness.

Luke 6:37-38 Reap what you sow; the implication is that we must forgive to be forgiven.

Romans 12:17 Be careful – do what is right – do not take vengeance.

Q7.

You have to practice it. Practice makes perfect!

Q8.

To describe what the Kingdom is like. Therefore everything important in the parable must be related to the nature of the Kingdom.

Q9.

Forgive (because you were forgiven). Since God has forgiven us for all our sins, we should in turn forgive others. It's possible that the debt that could not possibly be repaid has eternal punishment in view.

Q10.

Does not matter – there will be *serious consequences*. There is judgment if we do not forgive others.

Q11. We can assume that the king in this parable represents God. The debt is a _**huge**_ sum of money and forgiving that debt is an astounding act of grace. The point of the parable would be that since God forgave us (and it was a big debt that we could not repay) we should be able to forgive others. The judgment on the unforgiving slave likely represents eternal punishment.

Q12.
The church is not extending forgiveness or grace once the offender has repented.
Q13.
1. Prodigal Son – Father forgives.
2. Esau forgives Jacob.
3. Joseph forgives his brothers.
4. Moses forgives the Israelites.
5. David forgives Saul.
6. David forgives Shimei.
7. Solomon forgives Adonijah.
8. The prophet of Judah forgives Jeroboam.
LEADER: Maybe one of these examples would be good for an extended discussion during class.
Q14. LEADER: You might ask, "Does anyone need to share with the class, your situation? Maybe telling us will help you tell them!" Maybe someone in the group would go with you, if needed?

Lesson 3 A Jesus Follower is FRUITFUL

Q1.

Romans 15:28	Fruit = offering
Philippians 1:11	Fruit = righteousness
Hebrews 13:15-16	Fruit = praise
Colossians 1:6	Fruit = church growing

Q2.

Matthew 3:8	Repentance produces fruit.
Matthew 21:43	There are serious repercussions for not producing fruit.
James 3:17	Godly wisdom will result in producing good fruit.
Colossians 1:10	Good fruit pleases God.

Q3.

Matthew 3:10	There is judgment on tree (person) producing bad fruit.
Matthew 21:19	Fruitlessness brings God's judgment.

Q4.
Not "producing" something for the Kingdom.
Q5.
God expects and wants good fruit.
Q6.
We are called by Christ to bear abiding or lasting fruit.
John 15:8 Fruitfulness glorifies God and in particular IDs you as a believer to others.
Matthew 21:43 Israel lost its privilege because of fruitlessness. [God will remove His hand of blessing if we are self-absorbed, self-satisfied, and fruitless] Note: The fruitfulness goes beyond us individually – here the reference is likely to the nation.
Q7.
a. **OWNER**: God owned the vineyard.
b. **VINEYARD**: The vineyard = Jewish people, or maybe imply individual person. [see also Isa 5:1-7]

c. **FIG TREE**: Individual soul (probably Jewish)

d. **COMING OF OWNER**: The <u>coming</u> for fruit, the desire of God that they should produce good works.

e. **BARRENNESS**: The <u>barrenness</u> of the tree, the wickedness of the people.

f. **VINEDRESSER**: The <u>vinedresser</u> was perhaps intended to denote the Savior or the other messengers of God, pleading that God would spare the Jews, and save them from their enemies that stood ready to destroy them, as soon as God should permit. The vinedresser interceded for the tree, for another chance. Implication: last opportunity before judgment because of rebellion and unproductiveness

g. **DELAY**: His <u>waiting</u> denotes the delay of His wrath, to give them an opportunity of repentance.

LEADER: You might ask your group, "What is the purpose of the delay?" Ample time.

Relative to the vineyard, note that the owner had been "a long time" expecting fruit on the tree. For three successive years he had been disappointed. In his view it was long enough to show that the tree was barren and would yield no fruit, and that therefore it should be cut down.

h. **"CUT IT DOWN:"** The remark of the vinedresser that he might "then" <u>cut it down</u>, denotes that such a judgment would come and would be just.

Q8.

a. Useless (no fruit) b. Using up the ground or exhausting the soil.

Q9.

See Isaiah 6:9-10. Ignoring the imagery of the vineyard, the extended time would allow someone to see, hear, and understand the eternal message. And as stated in Isaiah 6:10, they could turn and be healed.

Q10.

We must repent while we still have a chance – or perish.

Luke 12:40 *You also must be ready, because the Son of Man will come at an hour when you do not expect him."*

Q11.

a. *__patience__*: Although God is patient, continual refusal is sure doom.

2 Peter 3:8-10 But do not forget this one thing, dear friends: With the Lord a day is like a thousand years, and a thousand years are like a day. 9 The Lord is not slow in keeping his promise, as some understand slowness. He is patient with you, not wanting anyone to perish, but everyone to come to repentance. 10 But the day of the Lord will come like a thief. The heavens will disappear with a roar; the elements will be destroyed by fire, and the earth and everything in it will be laid bare. NIV

b. *__opportunity:__* God treats sinners this way now: He spares them long; that he gives them opportunities of repentance.

c. *__uselessness:__* Uselessness invites disaster. Fruitless is not only useless to the church, but pernicious to the world.

d. *__use of resources__*: Many live but to burden their surroundings.

e. *__time__*: In due time, when they are fairly tried, they shall be cut down; Time is running out:

- The door is closing.
- The Master of the house is coming.
- Judgment or joy awaits.

f. _**judgment**_: The universe will bow to the awful judgment of God. Every knee will bow.

g. _**expectation:**_ Never was a nation (generation) entrusted with so much as ours and thus never was a generation so answerable to God. Where much is given much is expected.

Luke 12:47-48 That servant who knows his master's will and does not get ready or does not do what his master wants will be beaten with many blows. 48 But the one who does not know and does things deserving punishment will be beaten with few blows. From everyone who has been given much, much will be demanded; and from the one who has been entrusted with much, much more will be asked. NIV

Q12.

God expects us to take risks in our ministry (Parable of the Talents). The two men who doubled their talents were described as "good and faithful." They proved their faithfulness by taking normal risks that produced fruit. Are we being faithful when we continue to do things that do not bear fruit? We must be able to do whatever it takes to reach people for Christ and help Christ followers grow in their relationship with Christ.

HINDRANCES

Q. In the real world (in your life) what gets in the way of producing fruit?
Ans: Apathy; luke-warm relationship with Jesus; not participating in church; no Christian friends; not in a supportive small group community.

Q. What would lessen the distractions or make them go away for you?
Intentionality.

Lesson 4 A Jesus Follower LOVES ONE ANOTHER

MEDITATION
Following rules or circumcision, as in the case with Israel, as a sign or condition of God's acceptance, means nothing. What matters is be transformed into a new creation and demonstrate love because of your faith relationship with Christ.

LEADER: You might want to ask an introductory question at the beginning of you session, for example: "Is love risky? Why? Why not?"

**AGAPE** LOVE

LEADER: You may want to ask at this point: "What about that needy person who seems to always and constantly need/want something from you?"

Q1.
If love did not come from God, where would it come from? Self? The World? Others? Our love is a reaction to God working in our lives "causing" us to love Him and others. God, in some way, manifests His love in and through us. "_We love because He loved us_"

Q2.
1. Sports or soaps on TV; job; hobbies.
2. I am lazy, tired.
3. Others are not nice; mean, unloving people.

Q3.
1 John 3:10   Loving your brother shows we are real Jesus followers.
1 John 3:14-15 If not love – remain in death – not real believers.
1 John 4:11-12 Being a Jesus follower obligates us to love – that is who we are.

1 John 4:20-21 We are commanded as part of being a Christ follower to love our brother.

LEADER: Ask, "Do you believe this?"

Q4.

Not saved, we remain in death.

Q5. n/a

Q6.

Provide financial help – pray for – help with chores – comfort – encourage – mentor/discipleship – connected in genuine friendship – serve – forgive.

THE NEEDS OF OTHERS

Mt 25:35-36	Hunger, thirst, clothes, shelter, etc.
Romans 12:13	Hospitality (in OT).
Acts 2:45	Sacrifice , if necessary.
Heb 13:1, 3	Meet needs of prisoners.

Q8.

1. (a) Provides opportunity to walk by faith if you give out of something other than your excess (b) it demonstrates your faith, love , and obedience.

2. It helps the recipient.

3. It demonstrates the love of Jesus to the watching world.

4. (a) My faith is real; (b) I care.

Q9.

2 Corinthians 9:12	So overflow in thanksgiving to God.
Titus 3:14	Meet daily necessities – so not live unproductive life.

Q10.

Since the term urgent need is not used elsewhere in ESV, probably the meaning relates to doing good works. See Eph 2:10.

Q11. n/a

Q12.

It is a lifestyle, not a single act or periodic occurrence.

Q13.

Love is a serious requirement of God!

LEADER: You might ask, "What does gaining nothing imply?" Ans: My salvation?

Q14.

If love is present, it will make possible the keeping of all commandments.

John 14:15 *If you love me, you will obey what I command. NIV*

Love promotes obedience and the two together constitute the law of Christ

Galatians 6:2 *Carry each other's burdens, and in this way you will fulfill the law of Christ. NIV*

Q15.

Apathy, disinterest, messed up priorities, or just sin.

Lesson 5 A Jesus Follower SERVES ONE ANOTHER

Q1.

Jesus, the Son of God, has stooped to do one of the most menial tasks – one that was normally done by a servant. It was not done when they arrived (when normally done) but during the meal, after everyone else could have volunteered to do it. A dramatic lesson in humility! It demonstrated selfless service to others that would very soon culminate on the Cross. No self-respecting Jewish man would ever stoop to foot washing. The external washing of feet was a picture of the internal cleansing that was needed.

Q2.

As a model or teaching device. If Jesus can do it then we should do it; it demonstrates how to serve others in humility.

Q3.

Be blessed. Nothing you could ever do or think of doing is greater or more humiliating than God Almighty washing feet.

LEADER: You might ask, "What do you think it means or implies that they would be "blessed?"

Q4.

A slave or servant is not greater than his master. Nothing you see Jesus doing (the Master) is beneath you (as the servant). We cannot think we are greater than Jesus so that such work is beneath us.

Q5. n/a

Q6.

Ans: The simple answer is "Thanksgiving to God." But what does that really mean? Note that it says "many thanksgivings."

LEADER: Ask your group, "What do you think would produce 'thanksgiving' for God?"

Q7. n/a

Q8.

God really wants us to act in a godly manner toward one another and treat each other as a brother.

Lesson 6   Jesus Followers SPEAK TRUTH to ONE ANOTHER

Q1.

What one person does can impact the whole body. It can jeopardize the health of the whole church. If there are divisions, disunity, arguments, factions . . . they need to be dealt with. Truth must be spoken. Falsehood or sin does not impact just the persons involved, but all those around them.

Q2.

Proverbs 24:26 and Proverbs 13:5-6: Everyone appreciates honesty.

Proverbs 11:1 and Proverbs 12:22:   The Lord hates dishonesty.

Proverbs 13:11 and Proverbs 19:9:   Dishonesty does not pay

Proverbs 12:19   Honesty endures, but lies are found out.

Q3.

Lies can destroy reputations. Liars cannot be trusted.

Q4.

We are to intervene!

Bringing back means more than telling someone you know about their sin. We are to help them stop and restore their reputation.

Q5.

"Spiritual" probably means someone of faith. No one is perfect. It does not mean someone who is without sin. It probably refers to someone that is more mature.

Q6.

(1) It is not our job to go looking for the sins of others, (2) Our job is only to

point it out if obvious, (3) The purpose is to restore not condemn (4) We are not responsible for inflicting consequence or retribution, (5) Restore means to reset what is out of place or mend what is broken.

Q7.
Without offense; in humility. Remember, next month/year it might be you that needs restoration!

Q8.
Admonish: It means to speak in a way that expresses disapproval or criticism; strongly urge someone to correct their behavior.
SYN: reprove; rebuke; reprimand.
Again, this rebuke should be done with love and in a spirit of gentleness.

Q9.
Oppose him to his face, not by whispering in the shadows.
This is a situation where Cephas was clearly in the wrong.
Error and hypocrisy can impact others to sin.

Q10.
Matthew 7:3, 5 Look at own life. Fix your own life before you confront another. If your life is a mess, you have no credibility!
Colossians 3:16 Allow the Word of Christ to guide your actions; be guided by God's Word that is in us when we admonish.
Proverbs 27:6 Respond to those you trust; you can trust a true friend.
Proverbs 9:8 A friend or wise person will appreciate correction.
Proverbs 19:25 Correction from one you trust is worthwhile – gain knowledge; the wise desire correction.

Q11.
Get a friend they trust and both of you talk to the individual; maybe get a pastor involved if necessary.

Lesson 7 A Jesus Follower MAKES and TEACHES DISCIPLES
Part A – WHO IS A DISCIPLE?
Q1.
Maturing; improving; becoming better; gaining knowledge and understanding.

Q2.
The simple answer is to think in terms of a mature believer; one who is unified in spirit with Christ and His church. No one is going to be equal to Christ, but the idea here is that one is working toward that status. You have a solid understanding of the faith and are growing as a disciple.

Q3.
Excited; highly interested; enthusiastic desire; urgent; avid.

Q4.
The Greek meaning here is to learn, but to learn through use and practice – not so much through instruction. The learning is through doing! Thus, a disciple is one who has an attitude of involvement.

Q5.
To take action; to put into operation; to employ.
John 8:31 (The Truth Will Set You Free) *So Jesus said to the Jews who had believed in him, "If you abide in my word, you are truly my disciples*, ESV

Q6.
1. "You will know the truth" and it will "set you free" (Jn 8:32).

2. You will be able to intelligently discern what is true and what is false. The ability to know how to invest your life (career; wealth; pleasure; family; or service to God).

3. Hebrews 4:12 *For the word of God is living and active, sharper than any two-edged sword, piercing to the division of soul and of spirit, of joints and of marrow, and discerning the thoughts and intentions of the heart.* ESV

Q7. I am already committed and I want to go deeper, understand more, and apply to my life.

Q8.

Working very hard to support or accomplish something; very loyal to someone or thing. It's about having the right relationship with God.

Obedience: (1 Jn 2:3-4; Jn 15:10)

Seeking after the heart of God (Ps 63:1; Isa 55:6; Mt 6:33)

Knowing God (Jer 9:23-24)

Loving God and One another (Mt 22:37-39)

Trusting and Depending (Ps 62:8; Jn 14;1; 2 Thes 2:3)

Q9.

A Christ-like lifestyle means loving God, loving others, and loving self. It would involve: *a.* Study of God's Word; *b.* Prayer Life; *c.* Worship; *d.* Fellowship with other believers; *e.* Personal Growth/Maturity; *f.* Witness; *g.* Ministry Participation; *h.* Family Life.

The Beatitudes (Mt 5:1-12) describe the ideal disciple and his rewards, both present and future. The person whom Jesus describes in this passage has a different quality of character and lifestyle:

- The **poor in spirit** (who recognize their spiritual poverty) will attain the kingdom of heaven.
- Those who **mourn** (who are truly sorry for their sins) will receive comfort.
- The **meek** (those who have disciplined strength) will inherit the earth.
- The quest for **righteousness** will be satisfied.
- The **merciful** will receive mercy.
- The **pure in heart** will see and understand the heart of God.
- The **peacemakers** shall be called God's children.
- And those who **endure persecution** for doing God's work will inherit the kingdom of God.

PART B – MAKING and TEACHING DISCIPLES

Q10.

1:5 we **lived** among you

1:6 you became **imitators** of us (*us and the Lord*)

1:7 you became a **model** to all the believers

1:8 the Lord's **message** rang out

1:8 your **faith** in God has become known everywhere

NOTE: Discipleship involves time and energy. You do it out of love. Definition of discipleship: Investing my life into the life of another so that the life of Jesus may be reproduced in them. (Hope Baptist)

Q11.

2:7 Making disciples is like being a parent raising children. We must be encouraging and nurturing.

2:8 Making disciples involves sharing our life.

2:9 Making disciples demands hard work; while preaching to you.
2:10 We are to live upright lives (holy, righteous, blameless).
2:11 Making disciples is like being a father.
2:12 The ultimate goal is to live a life worthy of God (encourage and comfort).
Q12.
1. There is a lot of work to do!
2. We need to be dedicated like a parent is responsible for a child.
3. In the end it is very rewarding, particularly when successful.

Lesson 8 A Jesus Follower SHARES JESUS with the WORLD

Q1. No hope – they face eternal destruction.
Q2. Not every gospel conversations is necessarily going to be immediately fruitful. I personally prayed for a friend for 37 years before she was saved!
Q3. It is certainly appropriate to pray, but someone must tell them.
Romans 10:14-15 *But how are they to call on him in whom they have not believed? And how are they to believe in him of whom they have never heard? And how are they to hear without someone preaching? 15 And how are they to preach unless they are sent? As it is written, "How beautiful are the feet of those who preach the good news!"* ESV
Note in Mt 10:1-4 the disciples are immediately commissioned as workers; Jesus gave them authority.
Also note that these are ordinary men not, super evangelists.
Jesus chose, called , appointed and commissioned them and us.
Q4.
Mt 10 – Sends the 12
They are called, given authority, and healing power.
Go to Israel, not to Gentiles (After His death Jesus commands them to go to the "world").
Message: Kingdom of Heaven is near.
Luke 10 – Sends 72
They went two by two.
They were sent ahead of Him to towns where He was about to go.
Luke 10:9 *Heal the sick who are there and tell them, "The kingdom of God is near you."*
Luke 10:16 *"He who listens to you listens to me; he who rejects you rejects me; but he who rejects me rejects him who sent me."* NIV
Q5. Someone who proclaims the Gospel; someone who demonstrates a godly life.
Q6. Someone who leads someone to the point of making a decision and they accept Christ.
Q7. The fields are always ripe, particularly in these days.
Q8. John 4:36-38 (sow and reap) In verse 38 Jesus expected the disciples to be both sowers and reapers. The sowing and reaping can occur together; the reaping for the Kingdom is not a task for one group or one era – each reaps the benefits of it forerunners and succeeding generations benefit from our sowing.
Q9. Go where they are and be like them so you don't cause them to reject you for non-important issues. If they relate to you and are not turned off by

Are you right with one another?

you, they will listen – but only to a point. You cannot be engaged in continual sin and expect unbelievers to think you have any credibiblity.

Q10.
Acts 16:3 Timothy was circumcised in order to avoid needless offense.
Acts 18:18 In Corinth, Paul cut his hair because of a vow taken.
Acts 21:21-26 Paul and his disciples "purified" themselves according to Jewish custom and made offering.

Q11.
Paul did not invite them to church – He went where they were.
In Antioch he used the synagogue of the Jewish Dispersion (Acts 13:14-15).
In Lystra He addressed crowds in the open air (Acts 14:8-18).
In Athens he spoke boldly in the cultural center of Greece, to those well-grounded in philosophy (Acts 17).
In Jerusalem he obtained permission to address the mob that wanted to kill him (Acts 22).
In Caesarea (in great audience hall) he spoke to leaders (Acts 25:23–26:32).

Q12. LEADER: take a show of hands to see which one, if any, is the overwhelming problem – then talk about that in your group.

Free PDF
MAKE WISE DECISIONS

[Get the ebook version for 99 cents]

Consequences Shape Lives.

This book discusses the nature of decisions and explores eight essential questions to make better decisions.

You are a few decisions away from transforming your life. You can make better decisions! This resource has sections on what makes a poor decision, questions to ask yourself, traps to avoid, short and sweet decisions, the wise decision framework, and twenty ways to be wise. It also has a handy decision-making checklist. (12 pages)

Free PDF: https://getwisdompublishing.com/resource-registration/

Kindle ebook for 99 cents: https://www.amazon.com/dp/B0FG8NC53J

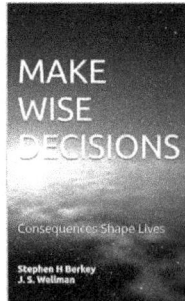

Ebook

Free PDF

Ten Steps to Wise Choices

Timeless Wisdom. Practical Tools. Lasting Impact.

Free PDF
Life Improvement Principles
[Get the ebook version for 99 cents]

You can live your best life!

Welcome to a journey of discovery! In case you have forgotten, your actions have consequences. Unlock your potential! This book (60+ pages) provides the overview of all our strategies and wisdom principles to live your best life. You *can* transform your life! Get your wisdom-based roadmap to a better life and unlock all the possibilities for growth and success.

Free PDF: https://getwisdompublishing.com/resource-registration/

Kindle ebook for 99 cents:
https://www.amazon.com/dp/B0FG883KZM

Ebook

Free PDF

Make it your life goal to be the best you can be!

Discover Wisdom and live the life you deserve

What Next?
Continue Your Journey

Continue Study in the *Jesus Follower* Series
The Jesus Follower Bible Study Series
https://www.amazon.com/dp/B0DHP39P5J

Be Challenged by the *OBSCURE* Series
The *OBSCURE* Bible Study Series
https://www.amazon.com/dp/B08T7TL1B1

Tackle Wisdom-Driven Life Change
Apply Biblical Wisdom to Live Your Best Life!
"Effective Life Change"
https://www.amazon.com/dp/1952359732

Know What You Should Pray
Personal Daily Prayer Guide
https://www.amazon.com/What-Should-Pray-Personal-Journal/dp/1952359260/

Decide to be the Very Best You Can Be
The Life Planning Series
https://www.amazon.com/dp/B09TH9SYC4

You Can Help:
SOCIAL MEDIA: Mention The Jesus Follower Bible Study Series on your social platforms. Include the hashtag #jesusbiblestudy so we are aware of your post.

FRIENDS: Recommend this series to your family, friends, small group, Sunday School class leaders, or your church.

REVIEW: Please give us your honest review at
https://www.amazon.com/dp/1952359627

The OBSCURE Bible Study Series

**Continue your journey through the hidden
wisdom of Scripture with the OBSCURE Series.**

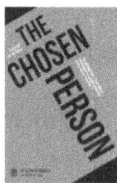

Blasphemy, Grace, Quarrels & Reconciliation: The lives of first-century disciples.
This book presents Joseph of Arimathea, Joanna, Ananias, Hymenaeus, and Cornelius (a centurion). It illustrates the nature and challenges of life as a first-century disciple.

The Beginning and the End: From creation to eternity.
This book has four lessons from Genesis and four from Revelation covering creation, rebellion, grace, worship, and eternity. God is leading us to worship in the Throne Room.

God at the Center: He is sovereign and I am not.
This book examines the virgin birth, worship, prayer, the sovereignty of God, compromise, and trust. God is at the center of all these stories. He is at the center of our lives.

Women of Courage: God did some serious business with these women.
This book examines the lives of Jael, Rizpah, the woman of Tekoa, Tabitha, Shiphrah, and Lydia. These women exhibit great courage and faithfulness. God used them in amazing ways.

The Beginning of Wisdom: Your personal character counts.
In this book we find courage, loyalty, thankfulness, love, forgiveness, and humility. Personal character counts. Decisions have consequences. Wisdom will help us stand firm in our faith.

Miracles & Rebellion: The good, the bad, and the indifferent.
God hates sin and loves to heal the faithful. The rebellion of Korah, Haman, and Alexander compare to the healing stories of Aeneas, a slave girl, and the crippled man at Lystra.

The Chosen People: There is a remnant.
This book concentrates mostly on Israel in the Old Testament, but also covers some interesting subjects as Lucifer, Michael the archangel, and Job's wife.

The Chosen Person: Keep your eyes on Jesus.
The focus is on Jesus and the superiority of Christ. We investigate Melchizedek, the disciples on the road to Emmaus, Nicodemus, and the criminal on the cross.

WEBSITE: http://getwisdompublishing.com/products/
AMAZON: www.amazon.com/author/stephenhberkey

Life Planning Series

Read these books if you want to live a better life.
The primary audience for this series is the secular self-help market,
but the concepts are Christian based.

	For the spiritual seeker and those with spiritual questions. *Your Spiritual Guidebook For Questions About Religion, God, Heaven, Truth, Evil, and the Afterlife.* https://www.amazon.com/dp/1952359473
	Core values will drive your life. https://www.amazon.com/dp/195235949X

Other Titles in the Life Planning Series
CHOOSE Integrity
CHOOSE Friends Wisely
CHOOSE The Right Words
CHOOSE Good Work Habits
CHOOSE Financial Responsibility
CHOOSE A Positive Self-Image
CHOOSE Leadership
CHOOSE Love and Family
LIFE PLANNING HANDBOOK A Life Plan Is The Key To Personal Growth https://www.amazon.com/gp/product/1952359325

Go to:
https://www.amazon.com/dp/B09TH9SYC4
to get your copy.

Personal Daily Prayer Guide
Prayer Resource and Journal

This is a great resource to kick-start your prayer life!

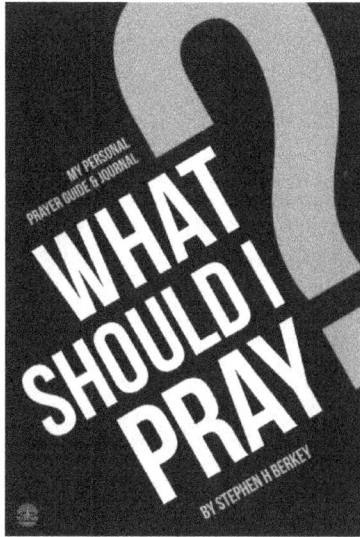

Know what to pray.
Pray based on Bible verses.
Strengthen your prayer life.
Access reference resources.
Pray with eternal implications.
Write your own prayers if desired.
Organize and focus your prayer time.
Learn what the Bible says about prayer.
Find encouragement and advice on how to pray.
Reduce frustration and distraction in your prayer time.

Get your copy today!

https://www.amazon.com/What-Should-Pray-Personal-Journal/dp/1952359260/

Acknowledgments

My wife has patiently persevered while I indulged my interest in writing. Thank you for all your help and assistance.

Our older daughter has been an invaluable resource. She has also graciously produced our website at
www.getwisdompublishing.com

Our middle daughter designed the covers for most of my books, but I gave her a vacation on this Series. We are very grateful for her help, talent and creativity.

Notes

1 *Practical Bible Illustrations from Yesterday and Today*, Richard A. Steele, Editor, copyright © 1996, 1998 by AMG International, Inc. ISBN: 978-0899572314

2 Christopher B. Adsit, Personal Disciple-Making, Here's Life Publishers, copyright 1988, ISBN 0-89840-213-1 (paperback).

About the Author

Steve attended church as a child and accepted Christ when he was 10 years old. But his walk with Jesus left a lot to be desired for the next 44 years. In 1994 he "wrestled" with God for some period of months and in September of that year totally surrendered his life to Jesus.

In 1996 he was so driven to study God's Word that he attended the Indianapolis campus of Trinity Evangelical Divinity School (Chicago) to earn a Certificate of Biblical Studies. His hunger for God's Word led him to lead and write all his own Bible studies for his small group. He has been a Bible study leader for the past 25 years.

After 25 years as an actuary, and 20 years as an entrepreneur, he began his third career as an author in 2020, when he published The OBSCURE Bible Study Series. The Jesus Follower Bible Study Series was completed in early 2025. He is a member of The Church at Station Hill in Spring Hill, TN, a regional campus of Brentwood Baptist (Brentwood TN).

"Get Wisdom Publishing is dedicated to being the trusted source of wisdom-driven books that inspire growth, guide decisions, and empower readers to live with purpose and fulfillment."

Contact Us

Website: www.getwisdompublishing.com

Email: info@getwisdompublishing.com

Facebook: Get Wisdom Publishing

Author's Page:
www.amazon.com/author/stephenhberkey

Amazon's Jesus Follower Bible Study Series page:
https://www.amazon.com/dp/B0DHP39P5J

"Go beyond devotionals.
Experience biblical wisdom in action!"

GETWISDOM
PUBLISHING

www.ingramcontent.com/pod-product-compliance
Lightning Source LLC
Chambersburg PA
CBHW060323050426
42449CB00011B/2630